The Secret Jewel

Peggy Morris

Table Of Contents

To my son Emil Morris

Acknowledgments

I am eternally grateful to all the people, family, friends, and mentors who have helped make this book a reality. It would not have been possible without your support, insightful guidance, and eternal words of encouragement. Thank you for being an integral part of this rewarding journey.

Introduction

"Until the lion learns how to write, every story will glorify the hunter."
—— *J. Nozipo Maraire*

Africa is full of immense potential and countless opportunities that have inspired visionaries and thought leaders globally. It is full of interesting history, different cultures, and fascinating stories just waiting to be discovered.

However, among the countless stories that have praised Africa, one viewpoint is often overlooked, kept secret like a valuable treasure, deep within the continent. It is the story of resilience, visionary leadership, and an unwavering commitment to unity and progress—a narrative that originates from a place I affectionately refer to as **"The Secret Jewel."**

In the journey of my life, I hold the honor of bearing witness to the breathtaking transformation of an entire continent, not just a nation. Amid this transformation, my homeland, a hidden gem, has somehow managed to stay under the radar. And while it may fly unnoticed for some, it holds its own in terms of size and population. This nation has remained a hidden secret, thanks to the lack of conflicts in the area, a smaller population, and most residents remaining within its borders. A lot of people don't realize that this country has always been fighting for unity and peace, even when those things appeared impossible. And even now, while some people may opt to be in the dark, there have long been some strategic investors, much like vultures, scanning the horizon for the opportunity. But both the leadership and the investors understand the vital link between being a gem and attracting value. They say, "Fortune favors the bold," and in this game of strategy, it is clear they are all playing to win.

Curious to know which country I am talking about.

The resilience and determination of the African people are on full display in my home nation, which frequently goes unnoticed by many. In this book, I want to share the incredible story of my motherland and its people. We have overcome many challenges, but we have remained unified and have never given up on our dream of a better future. "The Secret Jewel" is more than just a story; it stands witness to the triumph of the human spirit over tribulations, the power of visionary leadership in the face of uncertainty, and the commitment to unity and growth. Within these pages, lies the kind of enduring progress that holds the power to shape nations and inspire the world. As you turn the pages, we will embark on a journey together—a voyage that will take us to the heart of "The Secret Jewel", and reveal the invaluable lessons it offers, for not just Africa, but the rest of the world.

In the chapters that follow, we will explore the depths of resilience, the heights of inspired and enterprising leadership, and the unbreakable bonds that hold together the diverse tapestry of this remarkable land. I hope that, by the end of our journey, you will share in the awe and admiration I hold for my land, a hidden gem of immense potential—a land whose story is a testament to the indomitable human spirit and the capacity for positive change. But before we get any further with that, just as the foundations of a building are vital for its structure, this story will be incomplete without the history of the land of Africa, and the abundance of cultures and humankind that resides within its folds. So, without any further ado, here's to diversity within the nations, and a brief history that made Africa what it is.

Chapter One

Africa- An Intricate Web of Diversity

F or several centuries, Africa has been subjected to numerous misconceptions, often seen as one big country. Far from being just the wilds of jungles and deserts, the continent has always stood proud of its opulent diversity and contrast in cultures, vast natural resources, and economics. Just like it is not possible to construct a building without bricks, it is imperative to understand the characteristics and distinctions of all the different nations that make up Africa.

In this era, despite the amazing advancements in communications, travel, tourism, and the undeniable progress of globalization, it often saddens me to see that there still are many people harboring the belief that Africa is a country and that all the people from Africa speak one language. Regardless of the ample evidence, this paradigm of knowledge and negativity often permeates our collective consciousness. And so, as a proud African myself, I take immense delight in taking advantage of this opportunity to witness and share my contrasting narrative. Allow me to break down the foremost stereotype; Africa is *not* a country. It is a dynamic continent that is home to 54 different countries, each with its array of cultures, people, and traditions.

Did you know that Africa's population amounts to a staggering 1.3 billion people?

Therefore, does it even come as a surprise to know that, with this impressive population, coupled with the approximately 30 million square kilometers of landscape, Africa has long held its position as the second largest continent in the world?

The population alone makes Africa a potential market opportunity that should be hard to overlook. Not to mention the seemingly inexhaustible untapped potential the continent holds within its confines.

Diversity portrayed, Africa is home to various races, religions, and ways of life. Not to mention the many governance systems, the abundance of untouched resources, the wide range of social classes represented, and the number of languages spoken. This diverse landscape is truly unique. While on the topic of the different nations, it would be avoidant of me not to mention the trauma, and harrowing experiences, these nations have gone through, with varying degrees of severity. From apartheid to cruel colonization. From civil wars to outright genocides. The detrimental consequences of these historical events as they unfolded also differ.

But even so, the African people held steadfast and remained undefeated. So, while the very same nations withstood trauma after trauma, and stood resolute, Africa also boasts of economic diversity like no other. Be it the bursting resources of Nigeria and South Africa, or the emerging economies of Kenya and Rwanda. Africa is a pot of gold when it comes to investment opportunities. To take full advantage of this undiscovered potential, it is vital to understand each nation's strengths, weaknesses, and challenges of each nation, before local or international investors can reap the rewards. Apart from the ample market and investment opportunities, Africa's political landscape is, justly, as diversified as the people within it. From thriving democracies like that of Ghana which was regarded as the first sub-Saharan country to become autonomous and fight itself free of colonization to constitutional monarchies such as that of Morocco. Some nations are still grappling with the aftereffects of post-independence, while others have maintained stability throughout their existence.

Other nations such as Lesotho tend to reflect a balance between constitutional monarchy and democratic governance that comes with its fair share of challenges. Regardless of the controversies that may surround these accomplishments, one cannot ignore the efforts that the people made to get where they are today. And if the world wants to create, and maintain, diplomatic and business relations with Africa, it is imperative that these milestones be recognized and commended for what they truly are, a feat of resilience and strength.

Apart from the political advancements of this continent, the cultural landscape that it holds is as diverse as it is profound. With over 2,000 languages spoken across the continent, to the art and traditions that are unique to each nation, Africa is no second when it comes to talent and capabilities. From East Africa comes the intricate art of beadwork, a standing tribute to the history and culture of the Masai tribe and its people, which is as traditional as it is contemporary.

One cannot mention art and Africa without talking about the music that has emerged from the countries of Mali and the Democratic Republic of Congo. The music from these countries has paved the way for the creation of a separate genre and the production of global icons like the legendary Salif Keita. Not to mention the late Mariam Makeba, from South Africa, and late Oliver Mtukudzi from Zimbabwe, the two profound musicians who, through their music, made a global impact, forever engraving their names in the music history of Africa.

These icons used their music, not just for entertainment, but as a form of storytelling, and enlightened the world of the social happenings within the borders of Africa. Thus, as I, like millions of others from Africa, continue to embrace the richness of our cultures, within us fosters a true appreciation for traditions and heritage that seemingly defines each nation at its roots.

And despite the challenges the continent has faced in the past, I stand witness to the African spirit that only continues to persist and shine brightly in the face of hardship. I testify to the vast number of countries that have chosen progress over being immobilized due to trauma and have covered their journeys toward recovery, proving to the world that they are more than just some statistics. They are unconquered and undefeated stories of people who wore resolve and resilience proudly on their chests.

By stating these success stories, I in no way mean to imply that the challenges are done. Africa still faces monumental issues like poverty, acute corruption, crimes, and HIV. But it is imperative to understand that these issues are not confined to Africa, but rather, are part of seemingly every nation in the world. This narrative should not hide the vast potential of growth and development that this continent has to offer. The worst enemy here is generalization. While many a conspiracy might hold a grain of truth, the sweeping oversimplifications often forgo the rationale and cognition that went behind the actions taken by the individuals.

How beneficial or harmful are these false narratives that are so strongly associated with Africa though?

False narratives can both harm and help Africa. They frequently uphold prejudices that hinder investment and opportunity discovery. However, they also motivate people to fight prejudice and show the world Africa's potential. By spreading optimistic stories and highlighting opportunities, we can build a better, more equal future for the continent.

So, I would not be too off to state that recognizing the various characteristics of Africa is a matter of respect, along with strategy, in today's interconnected world. It is a recognition that asks for faith in the potential of possibilities that may arise. It is an acknowledgment that will work to form successful partnerships, and collaborations, that are unique to each country.

Whether it's in diplomacy, economics, commerce, or development, understanding Africa's diversity can unlock a wealth of mutually beneficial interactions. This knowledge can enhance both national and international relationships, paving the way for a more prosperous future. The world today is outspoken and unequivocal in its conversations of inclusion and diversity. And I am here to tell you that this very narrative applies to every single one of us.

As we embark on the adventure of discovering Africa's dynamic and diversified essence and identity, do so with a sense of understanding, an open mind, and a purpose to find the truth. Know that Africa is more than just a promise confined to the boardrooms of investors or the hallways of diplomacy; it lives and breathes in the heart of everyone of its descent. It is the force in the small enterprises that holds the power to drive local economies. It is the light in communities that never cease to celebrate their cultures and traditions. It resonates with the visionary youth, who are breaking the generational curses and have started to shape their future for the better.

Join me as we celebrate Africa's diversity and uniqueness, of each of her nations. Together, we can contribute to their progress and change the underlying negative narrative. Africa's promise is a shared one. It is not limited to its borders but ventures boldly into the rest of the world. So, ask yourselves; are you brave enough to join in, as the nations in Africa commence their journey towards a brighter future? A future that has its roots firmly in the recognition of its diverse and extraordinary landscape, be it cultural, traditional, political, or economic.

Chapter Two

Colonization: A Historical Legacy

Like every nation of this world, Africa too has a history as rich as any. And as many tales go, a part of this continent's history is shrouded in colonization that was powered by greed and materialism. History narrates that when the Western countries learned of the immense potential and the vastness of valuable resources lying aplenty, they wanted to take control of the continent.

And as an African, I can say, without a single doubt, that my people will never forget this gruesome colonization. It might be a happenstance in the history books for many, but for my people, it held severe consequences and changed the nation's course in drastic ways. Even now, when the world is changing, and proud of breaking free of existing biases that have haunted humankind for centuries, there are still many who look down on and mock Africa. What they refuse to, or are unable to understand, is that actions have consequences. And what Africa is now, despite its opulent advantages and diversity of people and culture, is the result of the very colonization and suffering that we had to face.

Due to the unashamed exploitation, extraction, and mistreatment of cultures and resources, at the hands of the colonizers, many African countries are still facing detrimental issues. The natural resources that were once plentiful were all used up for economic gain, leaving many a country in incessant poverty. A poverty that exists to this date.

But that was not where it stopped.

Further damage was imposed when the existing social structures were dismantled, and the Westerners chose to draw arbitrary lines, without considering the complex web of races and cultures, causing long-lasting disputes.

And if you look closely, you can still see the aftereffects in the form of economic inequality, governmental unrest, and seemingly never-ending social issues. To lessen the impact of this historical event, monumental work needs to be done, through an approach that is planned to the dot, inclusive and smart.

And, so, it would not be too far off to say that we must understand the continent's historical background and the problems it has faced and continues to if we want to work together towards a more fair and prosperous future.

Taking into consideration the current situation in the different nations of Africa, it is quite clear that to deal with the prevailing consequences of colonization, true dedication is required. A commitment to right the wrongs of the past. A devotion towards promoting the economic growth of this continent. A loyalty to reclaim the power taken from the nations of Africa. A perseverance towards the continued liberation of our people.

To venture off and fight the pre-decided fates, it is vital to be aware of, and truly understand, the history of the African nations. And once we do, we will be capable of more than just a simple change. We will be able to create a lasting, inclusive, future where the strength and diversity of the people of Africa, and its cultures, can once again grow, free of all constraints.

And then there is the Post Hoc Ergo Propter Hoc which can be summarized as "after this, therefore because of this" fallacy. It assumes that if one event follows another, the first must have caused the second. While colonization has had a significant impact, I believe that not all of the problems that are currently being faced in Africa can be traced back to it.

So, let's walk together, hand in hand, and aim to change the underlying narrative. Africa is more than just a collection of wars, problems, and issues. It lives and breathes resilience, resolve, strength, progress, and a dream to truly be free.

Did you know that the Berlin Conference of 1884-1885, also known as the "Scramble for Africa," was a pivotal moment in the colonization of the continent? During this conference, 14 European powers convened to establish rules for the division and colonization of Africa, without any African representatives present.

Chapter Three

Africa's Challenges

One of the biggest reasons behind the hurdles that the African people face is none other than the challenges presented by a lack of social infrastructure. Because of this very issue, there has been a noted decline in investor engagement due to the fear potential investors feel when considering business opportunities in nations that lack a social infrastructure. Despite the untapped markets of the continent, these astute investors tend to develop some resistance.

But not all the hesitation on the investors' part is due to the fear of underdeveloped infrastructure. Numerous African countries are still struggling because of limited clean water, while others are left hopeless due to inadequate road networks. Additionally, there are several more issues like intermittent electricity supply and the lack of fast internet, which by far, is the reigning predicament.

I met a woman on a bus not too long ago, and what started with a conversation about weather, ended up into a lengthy exchange on how humid the African continent can get. I casually stated my opinion of how I preferred cooler temperatures and could not tolerate humid climates. To this, she replied with a counter suggestion that the lack of clean water in Africa might be another factor in my decision not to live there, and I merely shrugged. Because there *is* clean water in my home country. And lots of it! Unfortunately, it is a common misconception.

This brings to mind yet another encounter I had with an elderly gentleman in a bus in Stavanger, Norway. As the bus crawled downtown through the gridlock, a slow rather interesting conversation started. As a person of color, I welcome the "Where are you from?" as an icebreaker of choice, especially when traveling abroad, and have gotten very used to it. As I was conversing with the elderly man, he frankly related stories from his time of residency in one of the African countries. He was employed by Equinor, which was then known as Statoil, a Norwegian energy conglomerate that had several operations around the globe. The man, who was now in retirement, proceeded to share memories of his youth and career quite fondly. It warmed my heart to see how happy he was, and how thoroughly he enjoyed his younger years.

However, I was quite shocked at his revelation of an incident in which a colleague of his, had been covertly embezzling money from the man's hard-earned pay, for over 15 years. He also mentioned that it had only been a few months since the police rescued him from this monster. I could sense his pain, his anguish, as he related his story and I wished from the bottom of my heart that I could have helped him during the hard times. The man did not elaborate further and out of pure curiosity, I even considered not getting off at my stop and staying to hear the rest of it, but I had some pressing errands to run. From what I had heard, the elderly gentleman, for whatever reasons, was being sabotaged. Hearing his story might have initially shocked me, but it came as no surprise.

Believe me when I say there are a vast majority of individuals in my home country who have not even heard of such stories. But, like many others, I too have been prey to such schemes. These stories are aplenty, and each dictates a harrowing event, including theft, pension fraud, etc. Some people, like me, had to fight hard to get back up, while many other victims, who no longer possessed the strength, ended up committing suicide.

The stories of the rich prince and the scams that have their roots deep in some African countries, and persist to this very day, come as no surprise. It's terrible and I wouldn't wish it on my worst enemy, but despite all that, I urge you not to generalize such incidents. Just like a farmer wouldn't abandon the entire crop if one of the plants died, it is unreasonable to condemn the entire continent.

Not all Africans are like that.

The world has paid a heavier price for the largest corporate scandal in US history, the Enron scandal, a little over twenty years ago. And yet, throughout the globe, new instances of fraud and corruption continue to surface. The fact that these challenges affect every single country makes them even more serious. As such, no country or continent should be thought of independently. These issues plague the entire world.

And in the last couple of years, I have had the distinct opportunity to travel to Nigeria multiple times. It was nothing short of an enlightening experience every single time. The biggest shock for me was the cultural difference, which was very pronounced, and I was not expecting that at all. This interesting piece of evidence portrays the immense potential that is rooted deep within the African continent. And the dispense of knowledge about the nations will break the perception of Africa being a singular country.

And while I empathize with the horrors that the nations within the continent had to face, it in no way means that immoral behavior is acceptable. Just like in any given situation, it is vital to address negativities to generate a productive ending result. And, thus, a harmonious and progressive future will not be possible for Africa, if the underlying issues are not brought to the surface and eradicated.

Cruelty towards others is just one of many consequences of the past and has the potential to, now, cause a ripple effect on the future generations to come. An effect that cannot be overstated. How horrible it is to think that a 70-year-old man, who dedicated his life and youth to working in Africa, had his entire life's savings lost to a con artist? The ripple effect comes thoroughly into play here, as this begets a negative connotation that becomes forever attached to the nation. And thus, this narrative becomes common all around the world.

If we look at the world, we will find that difficulties are a part of every country's journey, regardless of its location. And so, Africa is just like any other, having encountered its own set of challenges which were then dealt with resilience and determination. The continent's experiences should not be viewed in isolation.

Esther Hicks discovered that what happens in the physical world is caused by your ideas, thanks to Abraham Hick's teachings. One of their most well-known quotes states that nothing needs to be fixed. Everything is going perfectly. So, when you stand in your own acceptance that all is well, you will be surrounded with more and more evidence that everything is well. But when you are convinced that things are broken, that there is pollution, that things have gone wrong, or that the government is carrying out conspiracies, you get caught up in that vibration, and you begin to manifest that type of stuff, and then you say, "See, I told you that things were going wrong." -Abraham Hicks.

Although we do not know for certain if this can happen all the time, one thing is clear: our thoughts are powerful. The West is no different so let us avoid tinted windows.

The *Ease of Doing Business Index* helps bring forth the issues and challenges of doing business in different countries. And while corruption and an unsafe environment contribute exponentially towards the difficulties in conducting business in various countries, Rwanda has emerged as a leading African nation, accomplishing the 38th position, out of the 85 countries examined by the World Bank. And in a very close pursuit, came Kenya, at number 58, in both the 2019 and 2020 reports submitted by the *Ease of Doing Business.* The placements achieved by Rwanda are attributed to the progress made by its visionary leadership.

When Paul Kagame took over the presidency of Rwanda, in 2000, he worked to establish an era of transformation and changes that massively changed the direction of the nation's progress. Although the presidency has been nothing less than controversial, with several international entities unhappy with the rumored dictatorial aspects, the progress is undeniable. Although the controversies make Rwanda's story a bit complicated, the country's story becomes that much more interesting to talk and study about, especially regarding the socioeconomic changes and the distinctive government administrations.

Did you know that women in Rwanda occupy over 60% of all its esteemed parliamentary seats? It ranked 7th in the 2021 Global Gender Gap rankings, outranking many established countries. The country is similar to a phoenix, rising from the ashes of ravaging civil wars, genocide, and horrible challenges, to become a shining beacon of resilience and progress. In addition to all those accomplishments, Rwanda boasts various other attributes including a thriving coffee industry that is known as the best in the nation.

On the contrary, Burundi, another country in East Africa has long struggled with political instability, effectively preventing its rise as one of Africa's major economic centers. Despite the lack of knowledge surrounding the region, it is extremely evident that doing business amid the dangers of such a place is undeniably perilous, compared to a more politically stable country.

Back in 2015, I can vividly recall a conversation I had, when having dinner in Oslo, with a couple of my friends from another East African country. During our animated conversation, one of my friends received a call from back home and her facial expression was completely altered. The ambiance seemed to die down as she related hearing about the news of a political upheaval. An attempted coup in her home country had resulted in several people injured while some buildings had been destroyed. As shocking as the news might have been, I remember not being too surprised, as news like these, from areas like that, had become a norm. Therefore, there is no doubt that, ultimately, the risk associated with doing business within locations like that always acts as a major factor.

Not confined to just one, there are certainly many nations where fraud related to money has always been an issue, particularly on the part of people in positions of power, along with politicians. Corruption has long since been a major issue in Africa, due to which, the reputation of the continent has been suffering consistently. And to me, it seems this corruption is doomed to reign as long as there is a standing lack of behavioral examples that should be taught to children. Instead of inherent corruption and fraud, children should be taught the values of patriotism and pride in the diversity of Africa. And when people realize that their goals are the same, they will be more caring and mindful of one another, instead of fighting.

And eventually, there will come a time when these very people lead the continent towards betterment. However, as things stand, the countries are going to need time to rebuild themselves, and consequently, this results in a lack of investment capital from the Foreign

Direct Investment (FDI). This is the very reason why several African countries have stunted growth. But, if looked at as a whole, the majority of African nations are affected due to a lack of control over their resources, which is a direct result of bad leadership.

That being said, in the past few years, many reforms have taken place and several of the countries have been actively demanding a larger portion of earnings from their local resources. This does make me wonder if resilience like this can be another stepping stone towards making the continent of Africa reach its potential. Especially if these reforms weaken the hold of the Westerners, who have been taking advantage of the continent for decades.

As it is, there is still very much hope for Africa and all her nations.

Reportedly, in the year 2022, after decades of abusive exploration at the hands of multinational corporations, Burkina Faso decided to nationalize its resources and remove itself from the said companies. Consequently, several of the proprietors, instead of donating or selling the existing properties to the locals, which included vehicles and mining equipment, chose to destroy them in an act of anger. In my experience, foreigners have always taken advantage of the local resources and benefited from them more than the resident Africans ever could.

In Africa, they found ample resources, along with cheap labor, that they actively chose to exploit and abuse. And, under the guise of FDI, these very corporations ended up having more control over the continent's resources than the locals did. Under the inspired leadership of Interim President Ibrahim Traore, Burkina Faso is ready to make a remarkable impact on the global stage. With nothing but growth and development in mind, the nation is employing a vigorous and potent approach, something that has yet to be done. Since this nation is one of the top names when it comes to the production of gold, it is about time they capitalized on the revenue generated by the abundant mining and put it to use by addressing the copious problems of its people. If this is done right, the nation can then focus on important infrastructural issues like transportation, healthcare, local economy, and several other aspects. But, like many other nations in Africa, Burkina Faso, too, is constantly facing political unrest and instability. And even though the potential of a prosperous future seems not too far away, the prevailing risks associated can overshadow the opportunities. And risks like these have a way of turning a situation from bad to worse.

Be that as it may, history has always portrayed a domino effect behind every successful story of liberation and independence. And when it comes to Africa, our people have always been the epitome of resilience and strength. And from where I stand, as a result of these minor changes in nations like Burkina Faso, I can almost see Africa arriving at the pinnacle of success. It is undeniable that Africa is going through a formidable change. A transformative journey. And just like the moral of "Beloved", a story from our childhood states, *Slow and steady wins the race.*

Africa might be slow in its reforms, but surely, with the resolve and power that the people of Africa hold, the continent is bound to reach its full potential one way or another.

This reminds me of a job interview, during which I was asked about the trajectory of the future of Africa compared to that of Asia. After contemplating the answer for several moments, I chose to reply with facts.

"I'm not sure about the future of Asia, but Africa, right now, stands right where Europe used to, not too long ago. And as you might have guessed, the rest is history."

If there is one lesson that research on corruption can teach us about reducing it in many African countries, it is the importance of encouraging people to speak up about it and take serious action against the wrongdoers. The deep-rooted nature of corruption in many African countries makes it difficult to eradicate. Unfortunately, it has become a significant barrier to progress in any economic growth.

To assess the level of corruption in each country, the Corruption Perceptions Index (CPI) is commonly used as a tool. It serves as a sort of leaderboard that reflects public sentiment towards corruption in different locations. However, in the current era, a major challenge arises due to the widespread circulation of misinformation and fake news. This poses difficulties for tools like the CPI to provide precise results. Access to reliable data and the establishment of effective data collection methods prove to be challenging in numerous African countries.

While tools like the Corruption Perceptions Index have benefits, they also face certain challenges, especially in areas where obtaining reliable data is problematic. To truly fight against corruption, what is needed is to foster an environment of openness and sincerity. For the continent to move forward, African countries must commit to maximizing their inherent strengths and talents.

Additionally, some nations are home to smaller, isolated communities that may lack representation in overall population figures. Similarly, incidents of corruption can potentially go undisclosed for generations before surfacing. In certain situations, this is because offenders operate with such coordination that they can conceal misdeeds for significant periods. In far too many cases on the continent, those who dare expose corruption unfortunately face severe consequences, even mortal dangers to their safety. When wrongdoings ultimately come to light after long suppression, some who bear witness face the most tragic of outcomes. Reliance on statistics in such an environment would undoubtedly yield an incomplete picture. Numbers alone fail to convey the true human cost of suppression and intimidation that has long shrouded many areas in secrecy.

Even within the comparatively progressive society of South Africa, there remain unfortunate incidents of corruption that warrant careful examination. While some cases have certainly been scrutinized thoroughly, it is prudent to bear in mind that other underreported episodes may still surface given time. South Africa has long fascinated global audiences in many ways. During the uniquely turbulent period of apartheid rule, the nation stood at the center of international intrigue. The Boer establishment displayed unflinching resolve to cement Afrikaner dominance over all others within the country's borders. Simultaneously, they enforced rigid segregation between black communities and themselves with zero intention of compromise on either front.

It has been observed that though apartheid officially ended long ago, its legacy still subtly shapes today's South Africa in many ways. Nelson Mandela stood as a colossal figure who made immeasurable, sacrificial contributions towards realizing a just vision of a unified, post-apartheid nation. Through his formidable intellect and determination, Madiba guided the country from the depths of division to the early stages of building a shared future of equality.

His remarkable influence persists as an inspiration, not only for South Africans working to fully heal from the wounds of the past but for all humanity. Madiba's indomitable spirit of reconciliation, which burns eternally even after his passing in 2013, remains the brightest beacon lighting the way towards overcoming any society's darkest hours. His towering example reminds the world that through moral courage and compassion, seemingly insurmountable challenges can be transformed into hope. His amazing impact spans eras and geographies, leaving an indelible mark on history that ensures his legacy will endure across generations.

During my time abroad, I had an insightful conversation with the CEO of a large Norwegian investment fund focused on developing nations. I was curious why my home country was excluded from developing nations that should receive funding, as others with higher GDP per capita were included. The CEO explained their criteria required countries to have it within a specific range. Interestingly, though South Africa's GDP per capita is higher than my nation's, South Africa qualified for their investments. However, my country did not, as we exceeded the level they set - in fact, we are the only Sub-Saharan country outside of Mauritius with a GDP above their threshold.

I pushed back in our discussion, noting that among African nations, South Africa has one of the highest GDPs per capita. The CEO acknowledged the criteria was a long-standing political choice they had made, rather than purely economic. He conceded South Africa was an exception because of the close ties that developed during the solidarity fight against apartheid. In this unique situation, flexibility was required. Their criteria could unfairly penalize nations that have seen strong economic progress like my own, while still allowing room for special considerations, like the vital role South Africa played in challenging oppression on the continent.

I understand the desire to provide a balanced perspective. While South Africa has experienced both challenges and successes on its developmental journey, the harms of apartheid cannot be overlooked or justified. Unequal economic growth that excludes many does not constitute true prosperity.

Rather than focus on specific GDP statistics, we would do well to examine how policy decisions impact all people's ability to live fulfilling, dignified lives. All nations, including my home, still have progress to make in ensuring justice, opportunity, and well-being are shared by all members of society regardless of identity.

After I ran out of things to say, I realized I had to admit it. Apartheid wasn't all bad, even though most of it was. To be fair, there were a few good things that came out of it, even if they weren't that important. Some argue that apartheid led to infrastructure improvements in white areas of South Africa, like better roads, hospitals, and schools. Johannesburg today shows signs of significant progress. However, it's important to remember that this development came at a huge cost. Apartheid created a deeply unequal society, where the majority Black population lived with far fewer resources.

The significant contrast between urban progress and rural development is an undeniable reality, distinguishing Western countries from African nations. Western nations demonstrate a fair distribution of advancements and ideas across their territories, leading to overall improvements within the country. This inclusive approach fosters economic growth, reduces societal disparities, and promotes social inclusion.

By contrast, African nations generally have a large gap between urban and rural areas, where progress is centered in urban areas and rural communities miss out. Uneven resource distribution worsens economic inequality, maintains poverty cycles, and expands urban-rural divides. Rural communities lack access to healthcare, education, and infrastructure, which hinders their growth and perpetuates poverty.

And while the decision to have a South African parliament in Cape Town could be seen as a way for the Boers to create some distance from the black population. Cape Town is a bustling city with different types of people and a strong economy that is always changing and growing. Being in Cape Town feels like being in the lively spirit of

Africa, while also being surrounded by beautiful scenery that reminds you of Europe.

Additionally, Cape Town is a popular destination for tourists from all over the world who visit throughout the year. However, it is crucial to acknowledge that while there may have been certain advantages resulting from apartheid, we must not overlook the detrimental consequences of apartheid's violations of human rights and other associated disadvantages.

South Africa had the fortunate opportunity to host the prestigious World Football Cup in 2010, a chance that many other African countries can only dream of. As the proud child of a South African mother, I must say that during that time, all Africans and our country couldn't help but feel a tremendous sense of pride. The atmosphere was filled with unforgettable joy, and the excitement was palpable. Countless events took place, numerous discussions were held, and an abundance of reports were shared, all contributing to the collective celebration. Additionally, South Africa triumphed in hosting and winning the Rugby World Cup Tournament in 2023, marking another remarkable achievement to be added to Africa's list of accomplishments.

It's moments like these that make us truly proud.

Once, a young foreign doctor shared an intriguing story with me about an encounter he had with an elderly patient one autumn afternoon. The old man had sought medical assistance for a persistent cough that had been troubling him for weeks. While waiting in the clinic, he observed the doctors and patients around him and noticed a recurring pattern: most of the doctors who attended to him had accents indicating that they came from distant lands. When the young doctor finally entered the room to examine him, the old man expressed his frustration with a furrowed brow. In a somewhat impolite tone, he questioned, "It seems like we have an abundance of foreign doctors these days. Where have all the local doctors gone?"

The doctor paused for a moment, genuinely considering the old man's question. Rather than dismissing his concerns, the doctor leaned in and engaged in a polite conversation. "That's an intriguing perspective," he responded with genuine interest. "But have you ever pondered the possible reasons behind this situation?" The old man shook his head, admitting that he hadn't given it much thought beyond how it personally affected him.

The doctor proceeded to explain the complexities of modern medicine, emphasizing how globalization and technological advancements have facilitated collaboration among doctors from various parts of the world. He acknowledged the scarcity of doctors in certain areas and how hospitals and clinics are compelled to recruit doctors from other countries to address these shortages.

However, the doctor's perspective transcended the functional aspects and delved into the profound richness that diverse doctors bring to their community. He highlighted the interconnectedness of people from different countries, emphasizing their shared humanity. The doctor accented the significance of each doctor's work, stressing the fact that their contributions are valuable regardless of their country of origin. As the conversation continued, the patient admitted to gaining a fresh perspective and thanked the doctor for explaining it more thoroughly. He explained that this newfound outlook extended beyond his concerns and allowed him to recognize the beauty of a world that works together to promote healing. With a deeper understanding, the old man bid farewell to the doctor. His heart felt a bit lighter, and his mind more receptive. Amidst the sounds of medical equipment and the scent of antiseptic in that modest clinic, a seed had been planted—a seed of understanding, sensitivity, and the enduring power of meaningful conversation.

In the present day, the world bears witness to the significant impact of African professionals, as their knowledge and skills have yielded remarkable achievements in various fields such as economics, psychology, engineering, academia, and medicine. African physicians, professors, and individuals have not only enriched the cultural fabric of their host nations but have also played a vital role in stimulating economies and fostering innovation through their diaspora communities.

Among these professionals, African doctors have garnered high regard within healthcare systems worldwide. They bring fresh perspectives, specialized expertise, and a strong dedication to improving public health on a global scale. Dr Denis Mukwege is a Congolese gynecologist who won the Nobel Peace Prize in 2018 for his fight for justice for the victims of the Congo conflict. Along with that, he has been honored with the prestigious Wallenberg Medal by the University of Michigan, which is given to exceptional humanitarians whose acts of compassion for the good of the vulnerable and afflicted demonstrate unwavering dedication. He has many other awards under his belt. Dr Francesca Mutapi is another well-accomplished Zimbabwean professor in Global Health and immunity. In 2017 Mutapi was the winner of the University of Edinburgh Chancellor's Award for Impact and the David Livingstone Medal. She was also the winner of the Royal College of Physicians and Surgeons of Glasglow in 2016.

African scholars have made substantial contributions to the expansion of human knowledge and the emergence of new academic disciplines. In the domains of technology and engineering, African individuals have been instrumental in driving innovation and achieving breakthroughs that transcend continents. The presence of Africans in various industries fosters a more inclusive and global perspective, showcasing the immense potential of the continent while dispelling misconceptions. Through cross-border collaboration, these experts contribute to a more interdependent and interconnected world, generating synergies that surpass cultural and geographical boundaries. Radiation oncologist Dr. Cathrine Nyongesa of Kenya is one such case. With help from the University of Texas MD Anderson Cancer Center, she and her husband established a cancer center in Nairobi, Kenya. In the 21st century, the collective progress of humanity is propelled by the exchange of ideas, knowledge, and perspectives, leading to mutual advancements.

Indeed, an interesting trend is the movement of people from Western countries who opt to leave their home countries and embark on new lives in Africa. These individuals seek opportunities and experiences that may not be readily available in their countries of origin. While the numbers may not be substantial, the significance lies in the impact and motivations behind their decisions.

The decision of individuals from the West to relocate to Africa reflects their desire for a fresh start, driven by the appeal of diverse cultures, business opportunities, or a more relaxed lifestyle. While this migration trend may not be as extensive as some other global patterns, it signifies a growing trend of individuals seeking personal and professional growth beyond conventional Western destinations. The influx of Westerners to Africa contributes to the cultural diversity and economic vitality of the countries they choose to reside in or do business in. Expatriate communities have expanded as a result, enriching the cultural fabric, and contributing to the economic dynamics of the African nations they embrace as their new homes.

In an increasingly interconnected world, the decision of Western individuals to settle in Africa adds an intriguing dimension to the narrative of global migration. This trend emphasizes Africa's growing importance globally and shows that more and more people are interested in moving to Africa for both personal growth and to explore available opportunities. It underscores the growing significance of the region on the world stage and highlights the increasing appeal of Africa as a destination for personal and professional exploration and development.

Did you know that Africa is home to the world's largest desert, the Sahara, which is roughly the size of the United States? Covering approximately 9.2 million square kilometers (3.6 million square miles), the Sahara Desert stretches across 11 countries and features some of the harshest and most diverse landscapes on the planet, from towering sand dunes to vast rocky plateaus.

Chapter Four

My Unforgettable Adventures

"I, against my brother. I, and my brother, against our cousin. I, my brother, and our cousins against the neighbors, All of us against the foreigner."

-Bedouin Proverb

This book would not have come into existence had I not made the courageous decision to quit my job without having any other opportunities at hand. It has always been a dream of mine to go around the world, experience the diversity of different cultures, learn about their day-to-day lives, and absorb all the knowledge that the world has to offer. I have heard that people gain a tremendous amount of wisdom when they travel, wander, get lost, and find themselves somewhere, and that has surely been the case for me.

On my first day at one of Norway's esteemed business institutions, BI Norwegian Business School in Oslo, anxiety was my prevailing emotion. I was behind schedule because I had slept longer than desired. After taking a train in the wrong direction, I arrived at the school just in time for the opening ceremony to start. I was privileged to attend an enlightening introductory lecture delivered by a sociology professor on the varying complexities of the different continents around the world. He also touched on economics.

As you might have guessed, a rather significant portion of the discussion revolved firmly around Africa, and the unease the topic and negativity evoked was palpable. Even though I was excessively overjoyed at the aspect of studying abroad and getting lost in an unfamiliar lifestyle, the topic gave birth to a multitude of different questions in my head.

Have I made the right decision?

Why am I in a place where I feel attacked right from the get-go?

Are things always going to be this way moving forward?

As the lecture went on, the attention of the entire room seemingly fell towards me and my fellow African people, who all absentmindedly gravitated to the right side of the room. The guest lecturer enthusiastically spoke on the issues of poverty permeating the continent of Africa, and then proceeded to talk about the undocumented African migrants, periodically entering Europe. As he went on talking on the subject, I could not help but wonder about all the homeless and impoverished European nationals, from different European nations, who have resorted to begging on the streets of Oslo, with some not too far from where the lecture was being held.

It was a tragedy of thoughts. Having read so many good things about Norway as an affluent country, it was clear that the lecturer's comments made me wonder why he was overemphasizing African migrants and their poverty when affluent countries such as his own are also having the same issues.

Fast forward to 2023, a renowned Professor at OsloMet, Rune Halvorsen, talks about a "complicated image of poverty" in his Euroship project. And while the project focuses on the European continent, he further suggests that because of income disparities, poverty looks different across the continent. This is surely the case in Africa, but not many outsiders see it this way. Because of propaganda and smaller, impoverished areas of the country being highlighted many people who have never visited our country believe that poverty is everywhere, which isn't the case.

Back then, despite how the lecturer should have approached the topic, I kept thinking about those African migrants. I related to their hardships as they tried tirelessly to build a better life in Europe, even when my circumstances were entirely different. I was seated in a recognized Norwegian Business School that possesses a certain allure, one that may not necessarily align with the preferences of the average Norwegian individual seeking educational opportunities. It felt like I had somehow stolen the money or pulled favors to get a place there. Standing in the face of that, I found myself with a golden opportunity to beat the stereotype and let the world see my talent and achievements.

As someone who hailed from the Sub-Saharan region of Africa, as someone who represented it, I wanted to stand up and speak my mind in front of the whole room. With utter respect and regard, I wanted to point out the ignorance by highlighting the fact that the issues, that were being discussed so openly in the room, did not consider the unique circumstances, history, and dynamics that were a part of the continent. I wanted to state how crucial it is, not just for Africa, but for the rest of the world as well, to consider the fact that continents are made up of multiple countries. Countries with their histories and traditions and cultures, countries with their unique administrations, political challenges, and economies; just like Africa.

Sitting there, I had all these ideas running around in my head, but I could not put them into words. And it was later that I realized that, after being in Oslo for just two days, I had already been affected by the social norms and cultural nuances. My prowess and spunk, something that I was very proud of, were inhibited and impeded by my limited exposure and experiences in the new country.

It is human nature to be a little intimidated, being in a new setting for the first time. The surroundings and circumstances differ from what you are used to, and so the actions, on your part, might be considered different as well. And we all just want to fit in while we experience life to the fullest. Because it is so easy to be judged on something as trivial as your thoughts, opinions, appearance, or the way you speak. Especially when you belong to a 3rd world country.

In my opinion, as soon as people learn that you are an African, they will form opinions about you based on preconceived narratives. I can feel their mental wheels turning, forming assumptions about me. So far, I have yet to talk about my rich ancestry, because I never get to that part. As soon as people see the color of my skin, the speculations and presumptions become quite evident in the way they see me or behave towards me. I'm a well-traveled individual, and there were times I visited places where I was the only person of African descent. And in those places, I actively faced odd glances, less-than-subtle inquisitions, and outright staring. Suffice it to say, I was thoroughly uncomfortable.

As I have traveled the world, one memory has stuck with me: my trip to the Maldives a few years ago. Although the sandy beaches and gorgeous lakes at my final destination certainly made an impression, it was an unusual encounter I had during a layover in Russia that really stuck with me. In the middle of the hectic airport chaos, I was held for a thorough examination of my travel documents and passport, while others were let through immigration without a problem.

In the discomfort of the moment, it dawned on me: I believe the incident stemmed from underestimation. It is an unsettling truth that some are quick to judge based on appearances or origins. However, through this experience, I have grown accustomed to the reality. Despite the unease, I hold firm to my sense of self and heritage. It is a source of pride, a reminder of the resilience and richness of my identity. In a world quick to judge, I stand tall, rooted in my origins, ready to embrace whatever comes my way.

Today, there are widely common elements of racism that play out in the minds of billions of people every day. But sometimes racism is like a false narrative that people feed into themselves. Consider a Japanese tourist who, upon arriving in Kenya, experiences severe cultural shock due to their noticeable physical differences from the natives. One possible assumption they might make is that this is how all tourists to Kenya feel. The next person they tell it to also believes it after going through something similar. Despite concerns about its accuracy, this story continues to circulate.

And in a manner comparable to what Cathy O'neil says in her book "Weapons of Math Destruction", racists don't try to put their assumptions to the test using facts. Most people just assume these things are real and don't attempt to confirm them. All they do is take someone's word for it and act accordingly. The problem is that these stories might lead individuals to form unfair opinions about others, which can have devastating consequences. We must seek the facts and challenge these narratives. Doing so will help put an end to racism and create a better society for all people.

And even though most Africans and African American people face the most extreme forms of racism. It does not only impact them; it impacts people of all backgrounds. It is widespread and the fact that it can affect people from all walks of life should be clearly understood.

As I reflected on the universal impact of racism and ignorance during my business trip to Brussels, a memorable encounter served as a powerful reminder. While en route from the airport to my hotel, I

engaged in conversation with a Spanish cab driver who defied stereo-
types with his genuine warmth and curiosity about different cultures.

His sincere interest in people challenged the notion that not all individuals lack knowledge. When I disclosed my origin, he surprised me
with his heartfelt admiration for my country's good governance, stable
economy, and political stability. His genuine praise left me deeply
impressed.

I am now convinced that every individual you meet is like a new
country with its own unique history, adding another layer of detail to
the vast network of human relationships. Despite our outward differences, there is a fundamental reality that unites us all; we always seek
our selfish reasons. We may overcome differences and discover common ground in strange places if we can recognize and appreciate this
shared motivation. Remember, there is an art to it, and it's subtle, yet it
can turn enemies into friends and strangers into fellow brothers. The
encounter with the cab driver underscored the importance of genuine
connections in breaking down barriers and combating ignorance and
prejudice. It was a poignant reminder that understanding, and respect
can bridge divides and foster a more inclusive and empathetic world.
The memory of that encounter will surely stay with me for as long as
I live.

Epiphanies can be life-changing, leading to personal development
and a greater comprehension of oneself. Once again, my time at the
Norwegian Business School in Oslo highlighted this reality. While at-
tending a macroeconomics lecture, I was truly inspired by the professor's deep analysis of hyperinflation. His breakdown of a complicated
subject made it easier to understand, and the practical illustration he
shared was very relatable.

As we explored the topic further, the situation in Zimbabwe stood
out as a clear example of economic turmoil. Formerly recognized as

Africa's breadbasket, the nation quickly transitioned from wealth to turmoil. This harsh truth struck a chord with me, touching on larger problems of unfairness and disparity. Zimbabweans' economic hardships were reminiscent of the difficulties experienced by numerous Africans who had to flee to nearby countries, even at the expense of their safety and well-being. The combination of academic theory and real-world impact highlighted the importance of empathy and understanding in addressing systemic problems such as racism and economic inequality. This experience served as a powerful reminder that moments of realization can spark not just individual development but also a stronger dedication to promoting equality and progress.

Amid the twists and turns of 2024, inflation rears its head once more, driven by a convergence of factors beyond our immediate control, like interest rates and inflation. From the enduring aftermath of the COVID-19 pandemic to geopolitical tensions simmering in regions like Russia and Ukraine, and the ongoing conflict between Israel and Hamas, the economic landscape feels increasingly uncertain. It is heartbreaking to watch the wars, the horrible loss of lives, and the devastating impact on the people and the economy.

Reflecting on my academic journey at the Norwegian Business School, where I gained insights into the intricate dynamics of inflation, I am reminded of the crucial need to stay alert. While the precise path of inflation remains uncertain, the ripple effects it generates across economic policies and society underscore the necessity of adaptability and foresight. And while Zimbabwe's economic struggles amidst the broader global context of inflation, it's important to recognize the country's remarkable natural assets. Zimbabwe is home to the breathtaking Victoria Falls, renowned as the grandest waterfall on the planet. This majestic wonder attracts tourists worldwide, mesmerizing them with its sheer magnificence.

Perhaps the most interesting fact to know about this nation is that it boasts a rich array of natural resources, including the second-largest platinum deposit globally and abundant high-grade chromium ores. However, like many African nations, Zimbabwe faces significant financial hurdles and requires astute investors to unlock its full potential.

While sitting in the lecture hall, my thoughts drifted to thoughts of visions of leadership, where I could steer the course of economic destiny. Yet, amidst these dreams, I could not ignore the troubling truth that certain choices made by the Zimbabwean government then had led the nation astray. Decisions such as the Land reform and participation in the Democratic Republic of Congo civil war seemed to have disrupted the path to prosperity, resulting in a wave of economic hardship.

I recall my experience in Athens, Greece, I can't shake off the deep impression it left on me. The individuals I met made a lasting impact with their deeply felt sadness, which seemed to affect every interaction. From enjoying a cup of coffee in a lovely café to exploring the busy streets, a noticeable feeling of unease hung heavy in the air. The streets were busy with tourists, but it seemed as though the locals seemed distant, as though they were stressed.

I visited Geneva, Switzerland sometime during the summer, and I realized that quality of life and economic turmoil is something that cannot be hidden by just looking at the citizen. The Swirtze live large and the aura in restaurants is appealing. It's different from what I experienced in Greece. This experience reminded me that having journeyed through the numerous landscapes of Africa and traveling to different corners of Europe and Asia, I have developed a deep admiration for the unique qualities of the people in Africa. Their exceptional energy and unity are truly inspiring, acting as a source of constant motivation. Even when dealing with numerous challenges, such as financial difficulties or other obstacles, it's uncommon to find an African in a negative state of mind. The continent seems to radiate a contagious happiness, living up to its nickname as the "Land of the Happy People."

Stepping into Johannesburg's vibrant OR Tambo International Airport always feels like a homecoming, a comforting sense of familiarity that spans the entire continent. To me exploring various African nations brings about a feeling of connection, even though there are occasional cautions about risks such as abductions or trafficking. Despite the challenges, this adventure has been truly amazing. Many Africans are drawn to Western countries by the prospect of new opportunities and a better life. Despite the daunting obstacles encountered by migrants in pursuit of their dreams, their determination remains resolute. Unfortunately, some end up paying the highest cost, losing their lives in dangerous efforts to cross the seas into Europe. However, amid such emotional stories, it is important to acknowledge that this is not the case for all Africans. Some people choose to stay connected to their roots, valuing their cultural background and the comfort of family connections.

Did you know that Africa is the birthplace of modern humanity? The continent is home to some of the oldest evidence of human life, with fossil discoveries in places like Ethiopia's Afar region and South Africa's Cradle of Humankind dating back millions of years. The famous fossil "Lucy," an Australopithecus afarensis, was discovered in Ethiopia and is estimated to be about 3.2 million years old.

Chapter Five

The Footsteps of Explorers– A Jewel

D eep within the heart of Southern Africa lies a magnificent secret waiting to be discovered. It stretches across a vast expanse, around 965 kilometers in both north-south and east-west directions, with its eastern boundary extending to the very tip of the continent. As you venture towards the east and south, you will encounter meandering streams and remnants of a historic wagon track, painting a vivid picture of the region's fascinating past. To the west and north, the Kalahari Desert dominates the landscape, its vastness intersected by lines of longitude and latitude. On the eastern and southern sides, a river gracefully defines the natural boundaries, adding to the allure of this breathtaking location. And what is this hidden gem, you may ask?

It's none other than Botswana—a landlocked country embraced by South Africa to the east and south, Zimbabwe and Zambia to the north and west, and Namibia to the west. With its diverse landscapes and vibrant culture, Botswana eagerly welcomes adventurers, ready to unveil its well-kept secrets and marvels.

Are you ready to embark on an unforgettable journey of discovery?

If you never heard of a place on Earth where four countries meet, you are missing out on one of the planet's fascinating secrets. In the eastern tip of Namibia Caprivi strip, there exists a truly extraordinary location where this remarkable secret unfolds. This spot holds a unique distinction—it is the only place on earth where four nations converge in perfect harmony. Botswana, Namibia, Zimbabwe, and Zambia all gather here, each contributing its own narrative and cultural heritage to the vibrant tapestry of this place. It is a meeting point where borders blur, and stories intertwine, creating a melting pot of diversity and a testament to the interconnectedness of our world.

Several articles, including one from Big Think, however, cast doubt on this widely held view. On closer inspection, they argue, the so-called quadripoint splits into two separate tripoints. It is as if you were looking at the scene through a magnifying glass and suddenly saw details that transformed the whole scene. The argument for there being tripoints hinges to some extent on their reasoning that the two tripoints are separated by 135 meters. While it is important to consider differing perspectives, Cartographic records and geographic surveys have long supported the hypothesis of a quadripoint in Botswana around the Kazungula region. Serious investigation and supporting evidence are required for any claim stating otherwise.

And even so, the claim that a 135-meter separation causes the quadripoint to split into two tripoints is, to put it mildly, questionable. The fundamental idea of a quadripoint—defined by the convergence of four separate borders—remains unaffected by this small difference. Because small measurement errors are prevalent but do not usually change the basic topography of an area, it is important to consider the accuracy of geographical coordinates and mapping methods. Adding to the fascination is Botswana's notable claim to having one of the shortest borders in the world. If we look at its border with Zambia in Kazungula, it's truly remarkable how brief it is. This is precisely what makes the Kazungula Quadripoint such an exceptional place. It is where boundaries become indistinct, where diverse cultures intersect, and where the vibrant spirit of Africa shines brilliantly. It stands as a genuine crossroads of diversity and wonder, eagerly beckoning adventurers to embark on a journey of exploration and unveiling the hidden treasures that lie within its magical convergence.

The region of Botswana is renowned for its vast expanse of wide, flat, and arid desert landscapes, which encompass more than 70% of the country's total land area. This characteristic terrain has become synonymous with Botswana's identity. One of the country's most remarkable natural features is the Okavango Delta, a UNESCO World Heritage site that spans over 1,000 square kilometers. Situated in the northwestern part of Botswana, the Okavango Delta boasts the distinction of being the largest inland delta on Earth.

Think of a huge oasis in the middle of the Kalahari Desert, where crystal-clear streams meander through grassy, life-rich vegetation. This is Botswana's Okavango Delta. The Okavango River forms a network of lagoons, channels, and islands when it expands during its yearly floods. Elephants swim in the water, hippos soak in the sun, and a plethora of bird songs fill the air; it's a nature sanctuary. Indeed, the Okavango Delta is a true gem of natural beauty, a testament to the awe-inspiring power of nature. Its origins can be traced back to the highlands of Angola, where the Okavango River begins its journey. The delta's distinct environment is shaped by a network of islands, lagoons, and waterways, creating a breathtaking mosaic of habitats.

In his words, the President of Botswana, Mokgweetsi Masisi, says that the Okavango Delta is home to the world's freshest water. This water travels approximately a thousand kilometers before eventually flowing into the delta in Botswana. It is at this point that the great

Kalahari Desert finds respite, quenching its thirst and bringing life to the arid landscape. In Botswana, you can find the remarkable Makgadikgadi Salt Pans, which are the largest salt flats on Earth. These expansive salt pans stretch across a vast area, covering nearly 16,000 square kilometers during the dry season.

Next is the small village of Tsabong which holds its allure as a spectacular destination within Botswana. The village is a gateway to adventure, surrounded by golden dunes and rugged terrain. To the west of Tsabong lies Khawa village, known for its breathtaking dunes. These majestic dunes are characterized by their rusty-colored sands, constantly shifting and reshaping with the winds. Exploring the dunes of Khawa offers visitors a chance to witness nature's artistic handiwork and immerse themselves in the captivating beauty of the desert landscape.

Now let your mind journey to a time when the Western powers swept in with ambitious objectives to safeguard the spectacular landscapes and varied fauna of Southern Africa. The Protected Areas are a prime example of a successful wildlife conservation initiative in the West. However, not everyone was very welcoming of these PAs. Let me explain. Indigenous peoples, I would say the Basarwa or bushmen, also popularly known as the San in Botswana's case, have their sophisticated environmental preservation methods based on their extensive body of knowledge long before Europeans arrived. There was a strict no-touch policy regarding each tribe's totem animal. Also, to maintain harmony with nature, there were holy regulations regarding the time and species of game to hunt. Now, in the present day, another story is taking place. Even if it was done with good intentions, the Western conservation strategy has caused problems, particularly for the locals. What began as an effort to increase tourism and line colonial pockets has devolved into a chaotic struggle between human beings and their natural surroundings. Sure, money comes in from tourists, mostly from the West, but how can we strike a balance between tourists and locals? That has proven to be quite challenging. Tourism, which has been largely controlled by Western heavy hitters, has only recently attracted the attention of local people. So, although the landscape is beautiful and the animals are majestic, there is a story of traditional practices clashing with modern conservation strategies, an ongoing conflict.

With this base, the country's tourism industry continues to ripen. The region is renowned for hosting an exciting annual event known as the Khawa Dune Challenge. Each year, people from Botswana, as well as neighboring countries, flock to participate in this thrilling gathering. The event offers a range of activities, including quad bike riding, race car competitions, camping, and immersing oneself in a vibrant cultural atmosphere. Participants and visitors alike come together to enjoy the festivities, fostering a sense of peace and enjoyment throughout the event.

Botswana has several fascinating aspects that you have previously learned about. It would be negligent of me to not bring up the world-renowned Toyota Kalahari 1000 Desert Race. Botswana has established itself as a host for this event since 1991. This race has a rich history, dating back to 1975, and has become a legendary event in the realm of motorsport. It attracts competitors from various parts of the world who are eager to test their skills and endurance in the challenging desert terrain of the Kalahari. The race showcases the spirit of adventure and the thrill of motorsport, leaving a lasting impression on both participants and spectators.

One of the most talked-about UNESCO World Heritage Sites, frequently called the "realm of the ancestors" or the "Mountains of the Gods," is located to the northwest of Botswana is the Tsodilo Hills.

For the indigenous San people, these hills are very sacred sites with deep cultural and religious meanings. The Tsodilo Hills are adorned with over 4,500 examples of ancient rock art, providing a fascinating window into the region's cultural heritage that goes back thousands of years.

The Tsodilo Hills' unique geological formations, including the Male, Female, and Child Hills, contribute to their archaeological richness. The area is located within the Kalahari Desert region, home to a diverse range of flora and fauna. Conservation efforts are in place to ensure the preservation. Guided tours of the Tsodilo Hills provide opportunities to explore the deep connection between the local populations, their spirituality, and the ancient rock art that adorns these magnificent hills. Visitors, scholars, and students from around the world are drawn to this site to learn about its rich cultural heritage and to witness the beauty and significance of rock art.

One of the biggest and most isolated protected areas in Botswana is the Central Kalahari Game Reserve (CKGR), which is located in the region's unforgiving Kalahari Desert. To what extent does the CKGR encircle the desert of Botswana? An astounding 52,800 square kilometers (20,000 square miles), thanks to the country's effective conservation regulations.

This brings to mind an incident from my past when I connected with a woman on LinkedIn, and she found out that I was born and raised in Botswana. She seemed to have heard rumours about this country and was interested in learning more. So, as we were having an exchange, she informed me that Botswana is on her bucket list, but that the largely desert landscape makes her nervous about really going there. I found it funny, but I am no longer startled by these misconceptions, so I chuckled.

Established in 1961, the CKGR has become famous for its extensive wilderness, diverse landscapes, and plethora of wildlife. In contrast to the arid surroundings, the CKGR showcases wide grassy plains, ancient riverbeds, and scrub vegetation, against the dry landscape. These expansive grasslands provide essential grazing areas for a diverse range of wildlife, supporting a rich ecosystem that thrives in this seemingly harsh environment.

The Central Kalahari Game Reserve is home to a remarkable array of animal species, including iconic African wildlife such as lions, leopards, cheetahs, giraffes, zebras, and various antelope species. It is also a sanctuary for numerous bird species, offering a haven for birdwatchers and nature enthusiasts. Beyond its natural marvels, the CKGR holds immense cultural significance as well. The San people or Bushmen have inhabited this area for thousands of years, demonstrating their resilience and deep connection to the desert environment. They developed an intimate relationship with the desert and its resources, utilizing their extensive knowledge to survive and thrive in these extreme conditions. The CKGR is not only a wildlife sanctuary but also a cultural treasure. It encompasses various landscapes, ranging from expansive level plains to gently rolling dunes. One prominent feature of the reserve is the Deception Valley, which is a fossil riverbed. During the dry season, this valley becomes a focal point for wildlife, attracting various species and providing excellent game viewing opportunities. It is a remarkable sight to observe the animals congregating around the water sources in this otherwise arid environment.

Beyond the wildlife encounters, the CKGR offers visitors the chance to witness the captivating beauty of Kalahari sunsets. The vast open landscapes and unobstructed horizons create a perfect setting for breathtaking sunset vistas. Additionally, due to the reserve's remote and secluded location, the night sky in the CKGR is a sight to behold. With minimal light pollution, stargazers are treated to the tranquil beauty of the unpolluted night sky, revealing a multitude of stars and celestial wonders. Tourism in the reserve is managed with a dual focus on respecting the traditional ways of life of the San people and preserving the unique environment of the region. The Botswana government recognizes the importance of balancing conservation and sustainable land use within the reserve, and it is committed to achieving this delicate equilibrium. Visitors to the CKGR can embark on immersive safaris in this remote location. They can witness the abundant wildlife that thrives in this harsh climate and gain insights into the history and resilience of the San people, who have successfully adapted to the challenges of the Kalahari Desert for generations.

Did you know that Botswana is one of Africa's most politically stable and democratic countries? Since gaining independence from Britain in 1966, Botswana has maintained a continuous tradition of democratic elections, making it one of the longest-standing democracies on the continent.

Chapter Six

Pages to Screen: Books & Films

B otswana is well-known not only for its beautiful scenery and storied past but also for its literary achievements. Through their works, Botswana's writers have eloquently conveyed the country's spirit and culture, highlighting its history, customs, and struggles for readers. Among Botswana's literary greats, Bessie Head stands tall. Head, who was born in South Africa, relocated to Botswana in the '60s and wrote some of her major pieces there. The publication year 1968 brought her work "When Rain Clouds Gather," a moving account of political refugees and rural revitalization. Two of her other significant pieces, "Maru" (1971) and "A Question of Power" (1973), delve deeply into racial tension, exile, and identity.

Unity Dow has recently left her imprint on Botswana's literary landscape as a well-known lawyer, human rights advocate, and writer. "Far and Beyond" (2000), her first book, deals with gender roles and cultural norms. Dow's other works, such as "The Screaming of the Innocent" (2002) and "Juggling Truths" (2003), show her profound commitment to the challenges and victories of her community; they too continue to address important social concerns.

The literary canon of Botswana also includes the works of the poet T.J. Dema, whose poems are lauded for their lyricism and social critique. As a result of the widespread praise for her poetry book "The Careless Seamstress," she is now considered one of the most prominent poets working in Africa today. Lauri Kubuitsile is another notable character; she is an award-winning author of novels, short tales, and children's books, among other genres. "The Scattering," a historical fiction, shows how colonization and conflict affected the people of Southern Africa. Books like "Okavango" by David Dugmore and "The Okavango Delta: A Visitor's Guide" by Karen Ross offer detailed investigations of one of the most spectacular locations in Botswana, thanks to the country's natural beauties. These books showcase Botswana's abundant natural history by providing readers with a full depiction of the ecological importance and scenic beauty of the Okavango Delta.

Even now, Botswana is doing its best to foster the next generation of authors who will bring their people's history and culture to life via their words. Modern writers are delving into new genres and using unconventional storytelling strategies to keep Botswana's literary legacy alive and well on the international literary scene.

"The Gods Must Be Crazy," released in 1981, directed by Jamie Uys it is a comedy film set in Botswana's Kalahari Desert. It presents a direct comedic portrayal of the contrasts between the basic, nature-based way of life of the Bushmen and the challenges of the modern world. The film achieved significant international success despite generating controversy due to its use of certain stereotypical elements. Another film set in Botswana that captivated audiences was the 2000 Disney production, "Whispers: An Elephant's Tale." This film follows the journey of an orphaned elephant calf as she embarks on a quest to find her family. Like "The Gods Must Be Crazy," it also showcases the unique beauty of Botswana and offers viewers an enjoyable and heartfelt experience.

Indeed, the release of the movie "A United Kingdom" in 2016 brought significant attention to the remarkable true story of Seretse Khama and Ruth Williams. The film sheds light on the historical events that unfolded as Seretse Khama, a prince from the Bechuanaland Protectorate (now Botswana), and Ruth Williams, a British woman, faced adversity and prejudice due to their interracial marriage. One noteworthy aspect of the film is its authentic portrayal of the actual locations where the events occurred. By shooting in the exact places where the story unfolded, the filmmakers were able to showcase the stunning scenery of Botswana and London, creating a visually immersive experience for the audience. The contrasting settings of Botswana's natural beauty and the urban landscapes of London further emphasize the significant cultural and societal differences that the couple encountered.

Even though he was not born in Botswana, popular fiction author Alexander McCall Smith substantially impacted the country's literary reputation with his critically praised series "The No. 1 Ladies' Detective Agency." Set in Gaborone and starring the adored Mma Precious Ramotswe, this show has given a worldwide audience a glimpse into Botswana's daily life and gentle wisdom. It stands out as both a television series and a film adaptation. Inspired by a collection of over 20 novels this captivating production features the talented actress Jill Scott in the lead role of the detective. They have gained global recognition for their ability to showcase the country's beauty and distinctiveness.

Also, to make it to Botswana's Okavango Delta, you should watch the captivating Netflix series "Surviving Paradise: A Family Tale." Enjoy an exhilarating adventure into the African wilderness in this movie, where the delicate ecosystem relies on the contributions of all animals, large and small. Find out what the Batswana have done to keep this beauty safe from natural disasters.

All of these film projects highlight the country's amazing storytelling abilities, which have played a significant role in putting it on the global map. Filmmakers are naturally attracted to Botswana because it offers such a stunning backdrop for historical dramas and adaptations of beloved literary works. I mean, with those breathtaking landscapes and a cultural heritage that runs deep, it's like a dream come true for capturing enthralling stories.

Did you know that Botswana is home to the Maun International Literature Festival (MILF), a vibrant celebration of literature, art, and culture? This annual event, held in the town of Maun, brings together writers, poets, artists, and performers from Botswana and around the world to showcase their work and engage in discussions on various literary themes.

Chapter Seven

Championing Success: Stories of Glory and Victory

I f there is one common denominator between nations, whether in the western or southern hemisphere, it is the availability of minority groups. Even though they are often left out or forgotten, they make a huge difference in their cultural diversity and richness. They embody the complexity of human identity and how important it is for communities to be welcoming. They remind us that diversity is not just a buzzword but what makes us stronger and more interesting.

Even so, it seems like the international media often highlights stories about these groups, particularly those from Africa. Thanks to the internet, people now have a powerful tool to share their stories and experiences. The critical thing to remember is that it's not about where people come from or where they're located—it's about the dominance of the data economy. The international media has a way of showing us only what they want us to see, which can lead to stressful and misleading misconceptions. It reminds me of what Hans Rosling discusses in his book "Factfulness." Rather than falling into the pitfalls of intuitive thinking that lead to misunderstandings, Rosling emphasizes the need to use facts and data to gain a more accurate understanding of the world. If we want to make better decisions and have a more positive view of global development, he said, we need a fact-based worldview.

With these concerns in mind, the San people were one of the indigenous communities inhabiting Botswana before European explorers arrived. They predominantly depended on natural resources and encountered various challenges presented by the diverse environment of the region. Even today, the San people continue to exist in Botswana, although they have become a marginalized minority that often chooses to isolate themselves in rural areas. It may seem peculiar, but similar situations can be observed in numerous countries, both in Africa and the Western world.

If you search for the San people in today's interconnected economy, you'll often see them adorned in their distinctive traditional leather clothing. This attire, which typically covers only a portion of their bodies, has become a trademark of their culture. Contrary to popular belief, most Africans don't dress regularly in traditional leather outfits because of Europe's life-threatening winters. The San's traditional leather clothing, crafted meticulously from the hides of animals they hunted, serves as a whispering reminder of our earliest ancestors, the hunters, and gatherers. Each piece, adorned with intricate patterns and symbols, carries profound cultural significance when worn during traditional dances and special events.

Let us travel back to 1999, a time when the world was captivated by the Miss Universe pageant unfolding in Puerto Rico. The spotlight falls on Mpule Kwelagobe, who proudly represented Botswana on this global stage. In those days, Botswana had only two popular radio stations, Radio Botswana 1 and 2, and their melodies filled the airwaves across the nation. It is amazing how news has a way of spreading faster than sound, particularly when it carries the weight of history. During one of the parades, Mpule Kwelagobe donned the very same attire that encapsulates the essence of our rich cultural history. With grace and determination, she became the first African winner and the first representative from an unknown nation in nearly four decades to claim the coveted Miss Universe title. The news of her remarkable triumph reverberated across oceans, reaching the shores of Botswana like a triumphant melody.

That day remains etched in my memory, as vivid as if it happened just yesterday. The entire nation was enveloped in a radiant glow of pride, a feeling that permeated every corner of our beloved homeland. It was not merely a victory; it was a grand celebration that reverberated from the dusty streets of Botswana to the sun-kissed shores of Puerto Rico. We were united in our joy as if we were dancing right alongside Mpule.

With that victory, that outfit ceased to be just a garment; it transformed into a powerful symbol. It embodied our resilience, our rich heritage, and our countless triumphs. It became a thread that wove together a narrative transcending borders, telling the tale of a proud nation making history on the global stage. As we cheered, our jubilation wasn't solely for a beauty queen; it was a celebration of Botswana's indomitable spirit, one that echoes through time and is woven into the vibrant rainbows of our culture.

Through an analyst's eyes, Africa has emerged as a symbol of selfless endeavors, and Botswana perfectly exemplifies this. Some Western governments and organizations present themselves in Africa as charitable entities, but not all live up to their claims. However, some genuinely excel in their work. The San people of Botswana have caught the attention of various governments, including the Norwegian government through NORAD. It is a crucial development partner alongside other non-governmental organizations (NGOs) in the San community and other rural areas to help improve the lives of those in need. Whether it is providing access to education, shelter, or fulfilling basic needs, the focus is on helping these individuals who prefer to remain in their current, natural, and indigenous areas.

In the remote settlements of Etsha and Gumare in northern Botswana, a remarkable tradition has endured through generations. Women in these communities practice the ancient art of weaving exquisite baskets using Mokola palm and indigenous colors. The intricate weaving techniques employed by these women are deeply rooted in the region's cultural history. It is truly awe-inspiring to witness how they have persevered in continuing this craft amidst the rapid changes occurring in the world around them. The baskets they create are not merely decorative pieces; they embody the resilience and creativity of the community. These baskets are not only visually stunning, but they also hold a functional purpose. They find their way into homes, adding a touch of elegance and cultural significance. The revenue generated from selling these baskets provides a valuable source of income, contributing to the well-being and sustainability of the households.

Chapter Eight

A Brief History-
Bechuanaland

I magine taking a journey back in time to January 27th, 1885—a truly significant date in Botswana's history when a protectorate was imposed. Thus, the Berlin Conference in 1884 stands as a pivotal moment in history, where colonial powers gathered to carve up Africa as if it were a pie. The country underwent significant changes and transformations during this era. Amidst the negotiations, Botswana emerged as a highly coveted treasure, valued for its abundant resources. The imminent threat of German invasion loomed, prompting the British to swiftly secure their position by declaring Botswana as their protectorate. In the larger game of colonial power dynamics, this act was about more than just establishing territorial supremacy; it was a strategic chess play. The effects of these momentous events were solidified with the signing of an official decree on March 31st of that same year, firmly establishing Botswana's position under colonial powers.

But what led to this significant declaration?

The Germans were eyeing Botswana, while the British were occupying the country at the time. So, the British imposed a protectorate on Bechuanaland as to keep the Germans away. They could extend their power over the area while giving the impression of benignant and protection because of the protectorate status, which also gave a thin layer of legitimacy. While the British may have viewed it as a strategic victory, Batswana saw it as the start of a new chapter, one that would be filled with difficulties and fights for independence and self-governance. Colonialism spread its roots causing widespread economic, social, and political upheaval that altered Botswana's society for the better and left an indelible mark on subsequent generations. Despite everything that was happening, the will to persevere shone through. Instead of being utilized as interchangeable pieces in the colonial game, the people of Botswana forged their road to freedom and independence. The path ahead would be long and winding, but the light of freedom would shine through them all, leading Botswana back to its proper place among the world's nations.

Allow me to introduce you to Dr. Jeff Ramsy, an exceptional historian who has delved deep into the intricate history of Botswana. Through his insightful research, a fascinating story unfolds—one that reveals the interplay of ambition and geopolitics on the world stage. This chapter in Botswana's history was marked by conflicts over power and land, as the nation found itself entangled in the unpredictable winds of colonialism. Dr. Ramsy's meticulous investigation into this era shines a light on the intricate details of this complex period. Through his research, the story of Botswana during the colonial era comes alive, vividly portraying a nation navigating through the uncertainties and challenges imposed by external forces.

As a landlocked country, Botswana faced unique challenges in its geopolitical position, sandwiched between South Africa and Southern Rhodesia (now Zimbabwe), both governed by white-minority regimes. The complexities of Botswana's history during the colonial era are evident, highlighting the struggles, achievements, and foresight of its leaders.

Botswana had a tough time after 1895, fighting an uphill struggle against a South African corporation and Cecil Rhodes. However, leaders Bathoen I, Sebele II, and Khama III were determined to prevent the territory from falling into the wrong hands. Their precious minerals, including diamonds, coal, nickel, and copper, were at risk if Botswana's land was to be swallowed up by the South African conglomerate, so they begged the British for help. That is when their petition was granted. Today, a monument honoring these three chiefs sits proudly in Gaborone, Botswana's capital, as a constant reminder of the sacrifices they made to defend their nation.

Witnessing the consequences of Rhodes' policy in neighboring Zimbabwe inspired them, these chiefs were hell-bent on fighting back against any further incursions. As a result of their resolve and leadership, Botswana successfully traversed the intricacies of colonial rule and maintained control over its precious land and resources thanks to its deliberate decision to seek British support. It shows how crucial it is to have leaders with a vision to protect a nation's interests and sovereignty when circumstances are challenging.

It is no wonder that the careful preservation of their land and resources was of utmost importance to the chiefs and the people of Botswana. The boundaries of Bechuanaland, as Botswana was known at that time, were drawn with great care, taking into account the distinct territories of different ethnic groups within the region. This thoughtful decision played a crucial role in fostering unity among the diverse population and laying the foundation for the future nation. It is worth highlighting that Bechuanaland was classified as a protectorate, rather than a colony, which had significant implications. In the sense that more local control, less exploitation, and an easier road to independence were all benefits of Botswana's status as a protectorate rather than a colony. This differentiation aided in the preservation of its cultural legacy and made the transition to self-governance more solid.

Kgosi Khama III supposedly had the greatest following of the three chiefs. The Ngwato people he ruled were in danger of being overrun by expansion, which is why Khama sided more with the British. Strategically, thanks to his profound foresight and political gamesmanship, the Ngwato people were spared a more severe type of colonialism and certain annexation by the Boer Republicans in South Africa and Zimbabwe. He was the first king in southern Africa to be interested enough in his reign to inspire a biography. "The Story of an African Chief: Being the Life of Khama" published in 1893 by Mrs. W. Knight-Bruce was the first, while "King Khama, Emperor Joe and the Great White Queen" published in 1988 by Niel Parsons was the final known work, published more than a century after the first.

It is also important to recognize the significant role of Seretse Khama, the grandson of Kgosi Khama III, during a time when European nations were actively colonizing Africa to exploit its resources for their economic gain. As colonization posed an increasing threat, Khama became aware of the dangers and took the proactive step of leading Botswana into independence. He became the first President of Botswana. His leadership, characterized by a commitment to democracy, human rights, and sustainable resource management, set Botswana on a positive trajectory.

One beautiful day, I was strolling peacefully around the lake in Stavanger, Norway, when I unexpectedly bumped into a British gentleman. As one would expect, he struck up a conversation and inquired about my background. When I mentioned that I hailed from Botswana, he immediately asked me which tribe I belonged to, suggesting the Kgosi people. I was both amused and impressed by his extensive knowledge of my home country. I clarified that the name "Kgosi" simply means "chief" or "leader" and is not tied to a specific tribe. It was evident that Kgosi Khama had certainly made quite a name for himself.

During that time, it was unfortunate that many African countries did not have the opportunity to assert their rights as boldly as the leaders of Botswana did through their petitions. Or maybe Botswana just became lucky as it was already occupied by the British and they did not want the Germans anywhere near Botswana. Hence imposing the protectorate. However, the bravery displayed by Botswana's leaders was truly remarkable. In contrast, other countries either surrendered and lost control over their resources during colonization, or they fought back, often leading to devastating conflicts. These varied reactions had enormous consequences, particularly when it comes to the economic challenges many African countries face today. Those who chose to resist colonial rule often faced brutal punishments, enduring the harsh realities of being under foreign control. On the other hand, those who gave in and relinquished control of their valuable resources found their economies suffering as a result.

The remarkable spirit of leadership in Botswana has transcended its initial boundaries and has been passed down from one generation to the next, continuing to thrive to this very day. One of the notable aspects that truly sets Botswana apart is the peaceful transition of power that has taken place among its five presidents throughout its history. This is a clear testament to the strength and effectiveness of Botswana's democratic system, which is quite uncommon in many other African nations.

Did you know that Bechuanaland played a pivotal role in the fight against apartheid in neighboring South Africa? Botswana served as a

sanctuary for many anti-apartheid activists and refugees fleeing per-
secution, including members of the African National Congress (ANC)
and other liberation movements.

Chapter Nine

Feast of Flavors – The Food

In Botswana, the rearing of cattle has been deeply ingrained in the way of life for generations. It's no wonder, then, that meat holds a significant place in Botswana's cuisine. One of the country's beloved national dishes is Seswaa, a pounded meat dish traditionally made with either goat or beef, which is often served with papa, a type of corn porridge. It's a culinary delight that has been enjoyed by Botswana's people for many years. There are a couple more popular dishes that you'll come across in Botswana.

Chakalaka, for instance, is a spicy relish made with tomatoes, onions, and peppers, adding a fiery kick to meals. Then there's bogobe, a hearty porridge made from sorghum or millet, which provides a comforting and filling component to the cuisine. These dishes are often accompanied by a variety of stews and sauces incorporating locally grown produce like pumpkin leaves and spinach. The combination of flavors and textures creates a rich and diverse culinary experience.

Oh, I mustn't forget to mention Samp! It's a delightful dish made from maize that's cooked together with beans to create a wonderful balance of flavors. Samp is often reserved for special occasions and big celebrations, making it a real treat when it's served alongside pounded meat. The taste of samp is simply delicious, and over the years, the recipe has been refined and perfected. Some creative cooks have even started adding custard or butter to the dish, giving it a creamy and richer texture that's truly irresistible.

And let's not overlook the popularity of dumplings paired with beef stew. The combination of tender dumplings served with a flavorful beef stew is a real comfort food that locals and visitors alike can't get enough of.

When it comes to Botswana's cuisine, there's quite a range to explore, from the traditional favorites like Bogobe and Papa to more contemporary dishes like Boerewors and Samp. But there's one particular delicacy that stands out and piques curiosity—Mopane worms. These intriguing creatures have become a unique and interesting part of the culinary scene. Surprisingly, many people in Botswana not only appreciate the flavors but also rely on them as a valuable source of protein.

The cuisine offers a delightful array of dishes to tantalize your taste buds. From the comforting and satisfying Bogobe and Papa, made from maize porridge to the flavorful Boerewors and Samp, there's something for everyone. And let's not forget about Magwinya, a fried dough bread that's hard to resist. These examples just scratch the surface of the diverse and flavorful cuisine that Botswana has to offer.

During her visit to Botswana in 2011, Michelle Obama had the incredible opportunity to immerse herself in the vibrant culture and savor the delectable cuisine of the country. She had the chance to sample a range of classic dishes, but one in particular left a lasting impression—the renowned Botswana beef stew. This mouthwatering meal featured tender beef cooked in a flavorful tomato sauce infused with local spices. Accompanying the beef stew were a variety of traditional side dishes that truly showcased Botswana's culinary heritage.

One of these sides was Morongo, a nutritious leafy vegetable similar to spinach, which added a healthy touch to the meal.

It is often enjoyed alongside papa, a traditional maize porridge that provides a comforting and satisfying element to the dining experience. During her time in Botswana, Michelle Obama not only had the pleasure of savoring the mouthwatering cuisine but also fully embraced the local culture and formed meaningful connections with the community.

She visited the Mmabana Arts, Culture, and Sports Foundation. And urged the youth to pursue their dreams and make a difference in the world by stressing the value of education, leadership, and self-determination. The Botswana Baylor Adolescent Centre, which is a component of the Botswana-Baylor Children's Clinical Centre of Excellence, was another location she stopped by. Kids and teens living with HIV/AIDS can get the help they need at this program. The kids couldn't contain their enthusiasm at meeting her. And this trip left a lasting impression on both the people of Botswana, demonstrating the incredible power of food to unite and inspire individuals from diverse backgrounds as they shared some of the local cuisines with her.

We all know that food has a special place in our hearts because it has the power to connect us with cherished memories. The famous quote by Jose Andres, "Food is memories," beautifully captures this sentiment. It's a simple yet profound reminder that the flavors and aromas of our favorite meals can transport us back in time, evoking treasured moments and emotions. Food has this incredible ability to take us on a nostalgic journey, whether it's the taste of a beloved childhood treat, or the comforting scent of a home-cooked meal made with love. It goes beyond simply nourishing our bodies; it's about the connections we form, the stories we share, and the traditions we uphold.

Chapter Ten

Faith in Daily Life - Religion

When we reflect on Christianity and its fundamental principles of love, forgiveness, and selflessness, we find a guiding light that leads us toward goodness. In a society where these values are embraced and held dear, individuals become ambassadors of compassion, creating a community where acts of kindness thrive and the spirit of grace shines brightly. It's reassuring to know that when these principles are at the heart of a nation, a collective sense of benevolence emerges, illuminating the path toward a more harmonious and caring society.

It was a Sunday at my local church in Bergen, Norway, when a serendipitous encounter occurred, transcending borders and leaving a lasting impact on me. I found myself engaged in a conversation with a gentleman who happened to work for the renowned Norwegian conglomerate, Orkla. As our talk unfolded, I discovered something truly fascinating - his deep connection to my homeland, Botswana, through the charitable efforts of his company.

It was incredible to learn that Orkla, with its presence in Europe, the United States, and Asia, had been involved in meaningful initiatives in Botswana. One initiative, in particular, captured my attention - a collaboration between Orkla and SOS Children's Villages aimed at promoting oral health in my home country. The thoughtfulness and commitment demonstrated by Orkla in making a positive impact in Botswana struck a chord with me.

As we delved deeper into our conversation, the gentleman shared his personal experiences in Botswana, a place that held both humanitarian and business significance for him. He recounted his time spent in the country. What stood out were the vivid descriptions he offered of the people of Botswana—their warm hospitality, genuine respect for one another, and remarkable sense of unity.

It was the stories of those residing in the SOS Children's Villages that truly touched him. These children, who had either lost their parents or were abandoned, exhibited an unwavering Christian ethos that resonated deeply with him. Despite the hardships they had faced, their spirits remained unyielding, and their determination shone through.

Christianity has held a significant place in the culture and history of Botswana, with approximately 77% of the population identifying as Christians. The country is home to various denominations, including Anglicans, Methodists, and members of the United Congregational Church of Southern Africa. These religious institutions have played a crucial role in shaping the cultural fabric of Botswana by influencing their moral values.

Moreover, these churches have actively participated in social justice movements, standing up against apartheid, advocating for women's empowerment, and working towards poverty reduction. Their efforts have been instrumental in driving positive change and fostering a more equitable society.

In addition to Christianity, Botswana is home to a diverse array of religious communities. The 2001 census reported approximately 5,000 Muslims, primarily from South Asia, as well as 3,000 Hindus and 700 Bahá'ís. These communities contribute to the nation's religious tapestry, bringing their unique traditions and practices.

It's important to note that not everyone in Botswana identifies as religious, with around 20% of the population considering themselves non-religious. This diversity of beliefs and perspectives adds to the multicultural and inclusive nature of Botswana's society.

Chapter Eleven

Guardians of the Fields-Cattle

Out of all livestock, cattle exceed all other animals in Botswana, a trend that continues to persist to this day. Why do I feel compelled to bring this to light? Well, there was a time when the number of cattle in Botswana exceeded the human population by a ratio of two to one. And for many years, cattle have served as a valuable asset in the country, whether they are raised for their milk or beef production.

With its vast land and perfect weather, it's no wonder cattle farming thrived there. This led to a booming cattle business over time. Botswana earned a lot through selling beef, especially in the years right after it became independent. The Botswana Meat Commission, set up just before independence, was a game-changer. It made Botswana a major beef seller, especially to places like the European Union.

How did we do it? Well, strict rules for controlling diseases were implemented and the cattle industry was managed by experts, benchmarking from the best. This helped keep beef at the highest quality, attracting buyers from all over. Botswana faced some challenges, like outbreaks of foot and mouth disease and not being able to keep up with the standards of the European Union, which put a dent on the country's trade.

And nowadays, everyone's talking about sustainability. Countries like Norway are now taking a hard look at their trade deals, especially when it comes to things like beef imports. It's all about finding the balance between making money and doing what's right for the planet.

Botswana is a land of breathtaking beauty and rich biodiversity, but there's a growing worry lurking in the background in regard to cattle farming. Some Norwegian researchers point out that with these cows wandering freely across the land, they're eating out a lot of vegetation, messing up the whole ecosystem, and causing soil erosion. That is when you get to notice that the environmental consequences of cattle farming in Botswana extend far beyond its borders.

Norway is now taking proactive measures to address the environmental challenges associated with Botswana's cattle farming industry. One significant step involves discontinuing duty-free imports and promoting sustainable practices instead.

In a world where the fate of our planet hangs in the balance, initiatives such as these highlight the importance of ethical trade practices and sustainable development. Countries must take proactive steps in confronting environmental challenges, as these efforts pave the way for a more sustainable and equitable future.

Botswana, along with Lesotho and Swaziland (now Eswatini), once shared an institution, the University of Botswana, Lesotho, and Swaziland (UBLS). This unique collaboration in higher education was a symbol of regional unity. However, during Chief Jonathan Leabua's tenure in Lesotho, the government decided to nationalize UBLS, transforming it into the National University of Lesotho. This sudden move left Botswana and Swaziland without a university, sparking a new chapter in their educational journeys. Both countries quickly rose to the challenge, establishing their own universities and laying the foundation for a new academic excellence and independence era.

Batswana established what is today known as the University of Botswana by taking matters into their own hands. Being one of the first universities in Africa, this was an important milestone.

They did not seek assistance from other countries. They relied on their grit and resolve to come up with a brilliant idea to fund the University. Everyone who owned cattle was asked to donate one cow and this initiative was called, "Motho le motho kgomo," and it demonstrated a spirit of teamwork and pride in self-sufficiency. Today, the University of Botswana is where lots of influential people got their start.

But that's not the whole story, there is another remarkable story from our history that demonstrates our dedication to helping each other succeed.

Because back then, getting into college was tough, and Botswana didn't have special schools for fields like medicine and Engineering. So, the government made a bold move, they sent their best students to study abroad. With support from the government and driven by their dreams, these students went on a journey that changed their lives and those of people they met.

With hope in their hearts and a determination like no other, these brave students traveled to places they'd never been before. Their educational journeys took them to busy cities like Ontario, sunny beaches in Australia, and prestigious schools in England and the United States.

Even so, they returned home with more than just degrees; they brought with them aspirations and goals. Their goals were to have a global impact and bring honor to Botswana. Their scores weren't the only thing that set them apart; the opportunity to forge their path was crucial.

It came as no surprise that a significant number of these students chose to make the places they had grown fond of their new homes. Some felt a deep connection and decided to stay indefinitely, while others experienced a constant pull, returning time and again. They were captivated by the endless possibilities that awaited them and were eager to absorb the knowledge and wisdom embedded within the diverse cultures they encountered.

These individuals transcended their roles as mere students; they became ambassadors, carrying with them the dreams and aspirations of our country. They bridged the gaps between East and West, North and South, forging connections and fostering understanding on a global scale.

As a result of this enduring commitment, our country's dedication to nurturing talent continues to resonate across borders, serving as a beacon of hope and inspiration for future generations. It's not merely about the acquisition of knowledge or the act of traversing geographical boundaries; it's about the profound connections forged between nations and the unbreakable spirit that emerges from these experiences.

Many years later, Botswana's education system has undergone significant transformations. It's truly remarkable to witness the strides that have been made. An impressive 88.5% of adults now possess literacy skills. Moreover, since gaining independence in 1966, our country made the important decision to adopt English as the official language. This is a true reflection of a rags-to-riches story.

In recent years, our country has witnessed the establishment of numerous new colleges, and even a medical school, signaling a strong commitment to fostering academic excellence and addressing the growing demand for specialized skills and knowledge. This surge in educational institutions not only signifies the nation's dedication to supporting educational achievements but also aims to provide a diverse range of opportunities for students.

The proliferation of universities has played a vital role in making higher education more accessible to aspiring learners. It has opened doors to a wider array of academic disciplines, allowing students to choose from rich domains of fields that align with their interests and aspirations. This surge in educational institutions has become a cornerstone of our country's intellectual and professional landscape. By offering a multitude of programs, these schools ensure that students are equipped with the skills and knowledge necessary to thrive in a rapidly changing world.

The establishment of a medical school holds significant importance as it demonstrates Botswana's sincere commitment to enhancing healthcare and medical education within the country. This development not only provides a local option for aspiring doctors to pursue their studies but also contributes to the overall improvement of services and the establishment of a robust healthcare system.

Botswana continues to invest in its education system, and the establishment of medical schools and new colleges stands as remarkable examples of progress. These institutions not only facilitate the acquisition of new knowledge but also enhance existing skills. Their positive impact extends far beyond the classroom, influencing the growth of society, the economy, and the overall well-being of the entire country. By investing in education, Botswana is taking a proactive and forward-looking approach to prepare for the challenges and opportunities that lie ahead.

The emphasis placed on Information communication technologies training in Botswana's National Education strategy is truly praiseworthy. By providing comprehensive ICT training and ensuring that students in Government-owned schools receive free ICT devices, they are laying a solid foundation for the upcoming generation. These initiatives not only prepare students for the ever-evolving realm of ICT but also strive to promote equality by ensuring that all students, regardless of their background, have access to the necessary tools and resources.

In its pursuit of progress, Botswana is actively encouraging foreign investment to support the development of its educational system. The country warmly welcomes international partners to establish institutions specializing in technical education, healthcare, and notably, business schools. In doing so, Botswana aims to expand the range of educational offerings available to its students. These partnerships bring diverse perspectives, expertise, and resources that enrich the learning environment. Students benefit from exposure to global best practices and gain a broader understanding of the interconnectedness of the business landscape.

Chapter Twelve

Gems beneath the Earth-The minerals

In the quiet hallways of history, a significant event unfolded within the intriguing domain of geology. It was in April 1967 when a young prodigy named Manfred Marx made an indelible imprint on the pages of time. Engaged as a geologist for the esteemed mining company DeBeers, renowned as the world's largest miner by value, Marx embarked on a remarkable journey deep into the heart of Botswana's earth.

As Marx and his courageous crew prepared themselves to explore unfamiliar terrain, an underlying feeling of excitement filled the peaceful town of Orapa. With the dawn of each new day came a mix of optimism and the weight of the unknown, as their trip could alter Botswana's destiny. On one fateful day, as Marx and his team tirelessly worked on unfamiliar terrain,. A reddish Kimberlite, adorned with vibrant hues, concealed a long-held secret deep within the earth. The revelation was nothing short of astounding! After an arduous search spanning nearly a dozen years, the team had struck gold, or rather, diamonds. Orapa, the very ground they stood upon, held an extraordinary treasure trove of diamond deposits, stretching across an expanse that seemed boundless. The month of November 1968, aptly dubbed the "month of revelation," marked the moment when DeBeers shared with the world the remarkable happenings beneath the earth's surface.

This caused ripples of astonishment and fascination.

As expected, the wheels of commerce began to turn following the remarkable diamond discovery. Negotiations between the late Seretse Khama, a prominent figure in Botswana's history, and Harry Oppenheimer, the then Chairman of DeBeers, revolved around the crucial details of conducting mining operations and determining revenue shares. After careful deliberation, they reached a compromise: a 50% share agreement that would shape the economic landscape of Botswana for years to come.

This milestone agreement paved the way for significant economic transformations within the country. Today, the Orapa Mine in Botswana proudly holds the title of the world's largest open-pit diamond mine, a testament to the immense wealth hidden beneath the country's soil. In fact, according to the Economist in 2023, Botswana ranks as the second-largest diamond producer globally, surpassed only by Russia.

To manage the intricate diamond trade, the Diamond Trading Company Botswana plays a pivotal role. This entity holds an equal number of shares and is responsible for sorting and handling the off-take of the precious stones. Additionally, a quarter of the rough diamonds are allocated to the state-owned Okavango Diamond Corporation. This corporation conducts auctions to sell its share of diamonds, ensuring both transparency and a fair distribution of the country's valuable resources.

When we look beyond the often-skewed media portrayal of African countries, a troubling reality surfaces. It becomes evident that certain African governments have found themselves entangled in unfair agreements regarding their valuable resources for example Burkina Faso as stated earlier but then it later chose to nationalize its resources. Unfortunately, these nations have not been reaping the benefits they rightfully deserve. It appears that less informed and vulnerable nations became easy targets for deceitful promises, as their weaknesses were readily exposed with just a bit of investigation.

In the town of Selibe Phikwe, Botswana, a significant mining operation known as BCL (Bamangwato Concessions Limited) thrived for several decades. This mine played a crucial role in Botswana's economy as it primarily focused on extracting valuable resources like nickel and copper. Since its establishment in the early 1970s, BCL has become a cornerstone of the region, generating employment opportunities for the local population and contributing to the country's revenue through mineral exports.

The underground mines in Selibe Phikwe yielded substantial amounts of copper and nickel ores. These raw materials were then processed on-site, transforming them into copper and nickel concentrates. These underwent further processing or were exported to meet the growing demand for these valuable minerals. Throughout the years, the BCL mine operated consistently, continuously expanding, and upgrading its facilities to enhance production efficiency and meet the rising global demand for nickel and copper.

BCL played a pivotal role in spearheading exploration activities that ultimately led to the discovery of the Tati Nickel Mine in northeastern Botswana. With a grand vision of uncovering and utilizing the region's mineral wealth, BCL initiated geological studies and exploration efforts in the Tati District during the early 1970s.

During their diligent explorations, geologists from BCL stumbled upon substantial deposits of nickel-copper sulfide. To ascertain the size and potential of these mineral reserves, further exploration and drilling were conducted. Building upon this initial finding, extensive geological evaluations and feasibility studies were conducted, conclusively confirming the economic viability of the nickel-copper ore bodies. Subsequently, the Tati Nickel Mining Company (TNMC) was established to oversee the development and operations of the mine.

During the late 1980s, Botswana's mining sector achieved a significant breakthrough as the Tati Nickel Mine officially began its operations. This momentous event brought about a multitude of benefits for the country, including job creation, infrastructure improvements, and the generation of foreign currency revenue.

The discovery and subsequent development of the mine have played a vital role in bolstering Botswana's economy.

The meticulous geological investigations and surveys conducted by BCL proved instrumental in identifying and tapping into the abundant reserves of nickel-copper minerals in the region. This thorough approach led to the remarkable discovery of the Tati Nickel Mine in Botswana.

In 2016, a series of operational and financial challenges hit BCL and TNMC, leading to the suspension of mining activities. This unfortunate turn of events had a severe impact not only on the residents of Selibe Phikwe and Francistown but also on Botswana's economy as a whole. The closure of the mines dealt a significant blow to these communities and the country's overall economic well-being.

Since then, the government has been actively exploring options to revive the sites or identify alternative uses for them. However, substantial progress in terms of reopening the mines has yet to materialize. As a result, the Botswana government remains eager to continue to attract investors who can contribute to the redevelopment and revitalization of these mining sites.

An interesting aside though is that copper, a base metal, fell 12% in 2023 and is still predicted to fall 5% in 2024 as a result of declining demand, according to the World Bank. But in 2025, renewable energy demand will rise in tandem with improved global activity. According to equity research analysts, commodity demand will be boosted if the Chinese government raises stimulus. This is because China is currently the largest consumer of most commodities, including copper.

Infrastructural initiatives, buildings, and industries in these countries are pushing copper demand because of its importance in electrical wiring and power generation, it has seen a further surge in demand as nations such as the US and China shift towards renewable energy and electric vehicles. Therefore, it would be a fantastic opportunity for Botswana to bring its mines back to life.

In addition to its diamond production, Botswana engages in small-scale mining of various other minerals, such as gold and silver. Notably, the eastern region of the country holds significant coal reserves in the Mmamabula and Mmamantswe coalfields. To harness this resource, diverse coal mining operations have been initiated, to develop a robust industry for both local consumption and export.

Furthermore, nestled in Botswana's northeastern region near the Sua Pan, lies one of the world's largest deposits of soda ash. Soda ash has broad applications in industries like chemicals, glass manufacturing, and detergents. As a result, Botswana has emerged as the primary exporter of soda ash to members of the Southern African Development Community, shipping over 35,000 tons annually to other countries in the region.

Did you know that Botswana is home to the world's largest salt pans, the Makgadikgadi Pans? These vast salt flats, remnants of an ancient lake, cover an area of over 12,000 square kilometers (4,600 square miles) in northern Botswana.

Chapter Thirteen

Hidden Treasures Unveiled- Flora and Fauna

G rowing up in Botswana, I had the opportunity to immerse myself in our country's amazing wildlife. From mammals to birds, reptiles to aquatic creatures, there was always something new and exciting to discover. Learning about how these animals behave and the places they call home was like unlocking a whole new world.

Botswana takes its wildlife seriously, with strict rules in place to protect them. A lot of people believe Africa is just a big zoo where you can see lions and giraffes walking around everywhere. That's not quite how it works. Most animals prefer to hang out in the wild, away from prying human eyes.

This is where national parks come in handy. In Botswana, these parks are like safe havens for animals to live their lives without any disruptions. It's amazing to see how much effort goes into making sure they're happy and healthy. And let me tell you, going on a safari in Botswana is like stepping into a real-life nature documentary. You get to see these majestic creatures up close, doing their thing in their natural habitat.

Botswana's safari is second to none, rivaling even Kenya's famous safaris. And it's no wonder why people from all over the world, even celebrities like the late Elizabeth Taylor and late Richard Burton, choose Botswana for their vacations. Chobe National Park, nestled in the breathtaking Okavango Delta, is a prime example of the stunning wildlife Botswana has to offer. From zebras to elephants, it's a wildlife lover's paradise.

One of my earliest memories of exploring Botswana's wildlife was a family trip to Chobe National Park when I was 8 years old. We woke before dawn, to get a spot at the best viewing area by the river. As the sun rose over the treetops, we were amazed to see herds of elephants come down to the water's edge to drink and play in the swirling currents. One young calf cautiously approached the water and reached its trunk in, spraying water up with obvious delight. Nearby, a proud mother watched over her baby.

We spent the whole morning enthralled by the various animals that came to drink and graze. We spotted large pods of hippos lounging in the shallows, keeping a wary eye out for predators. Egrets and herons picked delicately through the reeds for breakfast. Further down, a family of warthogs rooted in the mud, little piglets following close behind their parents. By midday, the heat of the African sun sent most animals back into the cool shade of the woods to rest. Our guide told us tales of the different species and habits as we watched. It was an unforgettable introduction to Botswana's amazing natural world. The memory still puts a smile on my face.

In 2022, Botswana proudly hosted the inaugural Forbes Under 30 Africa Summit, marking a significant milestone for entrepreneurs in the region. This momentous event brought together a dynamic and enterprising group of young innovators, disruptors, and trailblazers, providing them with a platform to exchange fresh ideas and valuable insights. The vibrant capital city of Gaborone warmly welcomed the esteemed guests, setting the stage for an extraordinary journey.

The summit participants embarked on an exhilarating trip to the breathtaking Okavango Delta. This natural wonder served as a stunning backdrop for the gathering, adding a touch of splendor to the proceedings. Botswana, known for its remarkable landscapes and warm hospitality, proved to be an ideal destination for such an esteemed gathering.

What is the Okavango Delta, though? Picture yourself gently drifting along tranquil rivers, surrounded by verdant vegetation and enveloped in the symphony of nature's melodies. As the sun sets, the Okavango Delta transforms into a captivating tableau, with the water's surface shimmering with reflections and painting a vivid panorama. Every sense comes alive as you listen to the resonant roars of animals, the melodic calls of unfamiliar birds, and the rustling of grasses.

But the Okavango Delta is more than just a delta—it's a vibrant oasis teeming with life. Envision gliding through narrow waterways, where clusters of vibrant water lilies adorn the banks, all in serene silence. Your mode of transport is a traditional dugout canoe called a mokoro, expertly maneuvered by a skilled polar. The tranquility of the surroundings allows you to immerse yourself fully in the experience, connecting intimately with the natural wonders that unfold before you.

Witness the spectacle of elephants gracefully submerging themselves in the cool waters of the delta as the sun dips below the horizon, casting enchanting shadows upon their magnificent forms.

Imagine setting up camp beneath a blanket of stars, serenaded by the gentle whispers of the African night. As dawn breaks, you awaken to a breathtaking red sunrise and the refreshing scent of dew-kissed grass. It's a sensory immersion that awakens your soul.

For those seeking new adventures, walking among the islands within the delta offers a unique opportunity. Accompanied by knowledgeable locals, you can delve into the rich shades of stories that cast together old customs and the delicate balance between humanity and nature. These encounters provide a profound understanding of the interconnectedness between people and the environment. If your heart beats for wildlife, nature, or simply the tranquility of solitude, the Okavango Delta delivers an experience that surpasses all expectations.

As I got older, I continued visiting Botswana parks and reserves whenever I could. One summer during high school, I volunteered with a conservation project in the Okavango Delta. It was a life-changing experience living in the delta for a month.

Every morning our team would set out in mokoros polled silently through the maze of waterways. Our guide Poloko had an uncanny ability to spot wildlife, sometimes finding animals even before our spotting scopes could focus in. One misty dawn, he motioned for us to be very still. Emerging from the fog, we saw a massive bull elephant with magnificent towering tusks padding towards the river for a drink.

We held our breath as the solitary elephant sniffed the air, no doubt catching our scents on the breeze. For a tense moment, it stared in our direction. Then, seeming to decide we posed no threat, it submerged its trunk in the brown water. Our guide whispered that well-grown tusks like that were a rare sight, and this elephant had surely faced many dangers to attain such an age. I'll never forget watching its stately form disappear back into the mists, a solitary monarch of the delta.

Such special sightings reinforced for me why conservation efforts in places like the Okavango Delta were so important. By protecting habitats and enforcing anti-poaching measures, future generations could also experience encounters with fully mature wildlife like that bull elephant.

The Okavango Delta has had the privilege of hosting esteemed individuals, including the likes of Prince Harry of England and the Duchess of Sussex. This enchanting destination has captured their hearts, prompting them to make multiple visits to its captivating landscapes. Their affection for the Botswana safari experience was palpable, with the prince expressing a strong desire for an extended stay in this mesmerizing locale. The Okavango Delta possesses a unique allure, fostering an environment that ignites love, forges deep connections, and inspires profound introspection. Their fondness for the region eventually culminated in a momentous decision, as they chose to celebrate their union and exchange vows in this remarkable land, a year after their initial encounters.

In his heartfelt book, "The Spare," Prince Harry describes Botswana as the very birthplace of humanity. He paints a vivid picture of a nation that stands as one of the most sparsely populated on our planet—a true sanctuary where nature reigns supreme. Botswana, he declares, is a veritable garden of Eden, with a staggering 40 percent of its land dedicated to preserving its natural wonders. But beyond its remarkable landscapes, Prince Harry reveals a deeper connection he shares with this enchanting land. Botswana is a place where he discovered himself, where he consistently rediscovered his true essence, and where he always felt an indescribable closeness to magic. With a touch of enchantment in his words, he extends an invitation to Meghan. If she shares a fascination for the mystical, Prince Harry encourages her to embark on this journey together—to witness the spectacle of a starlit sky.

During their exploration of Botswana's breathtaking landscapes, Prince Harry and Meghan made thoughtful choices in selecting their accommodations, opting for prestigious establishments such as the renowned Mapula Lodge. This exquisite lodge is strategically nestled within the Okavango Delta, offering them a prime location to immerse themselves in the delta's natural wonders.

Prince Harry's connection to Botswana goes beyond mere visits. His time in this remarkable country has been marked by a passionate dedication to philanthropic endeavors. Collaborating closely with esteemed non-governmental organizations (NGOs), he has committed himself to making a positive impact on the lives of young children. This noble pursuit resonates deeply with his core values and aspirations, reflecting his genuine desire to uplift and empower the next generation.

As if a gentle breeze were heralding the coming of a Hollywood icon, Botswana was full of excitement in the middle of 2023. The news that the talented Will Smith was coming to town spread like wildfire, igniting a frenzy of anticipation across the country. Every day brought him closer, and the air crackled with excitement as people eagerly waited for his arrival.

When the moment finally came, it was like magic. As the sun dipped below the horizon, hearts raced with anticipation as he stepped onto the grounds of Sir Seretse Khama International Airport. His smile lit up the night, matching the brilliance of the African sun.

With boundless energy, the 54-year-old star dove headfirst into the adventure, starting with a thrilling safari in the untamed beauty of Botswana's Okavango Delta. It was a moment to remember as he marveled at the wonders of the wildlife, soaking in the magic of the African wilderness.

The Okavango Delta isn't just a hotspot for safaris anymore – it is also a buzzing hub for business ventures. Here, world-renowned business magnates from all over the globe gather to network and check out investment opportunities. Botswana is already an unforgettable destination, and its commitment to facilitating the success of international firms is just icing on the cake.

One of the big names who saw the potential in Botswana was none other than Sir Richard Branson, the brains behind the Virgin Group. He resolved to personally investigate the expanding opportunities in this land of possibility. Branson went so far as to attend the 2017 Global Expo, where he met other curious minds anxious to explore what Botswana had to offer.

Did you know that Botswana's Kalahari Desert is not a true desert in the traditional sense, but rather a semi-arid sandy savanna? Despite its classification, the Kalahari supports a surprising variety of plant and animal life, including unique species adapted to its harsh conditions.

Chapter Fourteen

Trunk Tales- The Elephants

D id you know that wildlife management initiatives and community partnerships can help make a monumental difference in animals' lives?

Trunk Tales has stated that the highest number of African elephants in the world live in Botswana. The impetus behind it is the ample advancement in wildlife management initiatives, impregnable conservation legislation, and prodigious community partnerships, all leading to an ideal environment for them to thrive. Largely attributed to the peaceful atmosphere of the country, despite the semi-arid climate, the number of elephants continues to grow at a steady pace. Although Botswana might be considered a haven for these majestic mammals, several issues have come to the surface, ascribed to their escalating numbers. Many debates have occurred on relaxing the terms surrounding the prohibition on hunting these elephants. Due to their large numbers, it is hard to keep them confined, which has resulted in these animals destroying people's crops and property. Not to mention the fact that, in recent years, these attacks have started being directed at people, leading to fatal consequences.

Because of this, in 2014, the hunting ban was lifted, implementing a shoot-to-kill policy. However, as the administration changed, this decision was vetoed, bringing the hunting ban back into place. Many have speculated on the reason behind this decision, with the majority attributing it to factors like trophy hunting and poaching for tusks. The decision to ban hunting might have been a humane one, however, the attacks by the elephants resumed, leading to increasingly austere consequences. In 2019, the government reported multiple deaths, including those of tourists, which led to a huge global upheaval. So much so that the current president, President Mokgweetsi Masisi, upon an official visit to Las Vegas, was asked point blank about this issue. His answer, centering around the inhumanity of slaughtering elephants, sparked several more debates about the safety of these animals versus humans, resulting in an array of different opinions.

Regardless of the outcry, Botswana has always held its place as the savior of these animals by adopting various methods to protect them. It might be shocking to some, but Botswana regularly donates these African Elephants to other countries that might lack in general diversity of the said genus. A number of protection programs have started because of overpopulation, with the sole aim of protecting these beautiful creatures. These are the very programs and conservation groups that aid international conservation efforts by providing a safe and protected passage of these elephants to countries all around the world.

Did you know that Botswana's elephants are known for their incredible intelligence and complex social structures? These majestic creatures exhibit behaviors such as empathy, grief, and cooperation, making them one of the most socially sophisticated animals on the planet.

Chapter Fifteen

Long Walk to Wealth

As far as 1980s global economic woes go, Botswana was up there with the worst of them. A roughly ten-kilometer-long paved road was all that was available; there was no further infrastructure. It was the cattle that were the primary contributor to the economy. Despite these obstacles, the path to victory appeared far, and the future held many more tests. Even after declaring independence from the Bechuanaland British Protectorate on September 30th, 1966, Botswana remained economically impoverished. Even though Botswana gained its independence, the countrymen were still unsure of its success, which added another layer of difficulty. Even though they were aware it would improve their lives, to them it was a completely alien idea.

Turning the dream of independence into a practical reality was a tough undertaking that Seretse confronted as Botswana transitioned from British authority to independence. There were several bumps along the way. The first few years after independence were quite difficult financially, said Molosiwa Selepeng, a former public servant. Botswana had a hard time keeping its recurring budget balanced for the first half of the decade. During this time, the British stepped in to help Botswana out financially, covering half of the country's recurring budget. However, Botswana's tenacity and resolve were evident even in the face of these initial challenges. The nation's fiscal situation had improved greatly by 1972. Botswana was finally able to take charge of its own budget management after years of meticulous planning and calculated decisions.

Squeezed between two minority-ruled republics, Khama found himself in a difficult position. Envision yourself as the lone duck in a lake where swans abound and you can't turn to any of them, that's the position Khama found himself in! However, that didn't discourage Khama. The independence of Botswana and the geopolitical constraints were no match for him. They could have used some assistance to keep things from sinking. They therefore cast a broad net for foreign aid and resorted to the Non-Aligned Movement. Surprisingly, European nations poured money into Botswana through direct foreign investment, helping the country weather the storms of international relations, and things kept getting better. Like his great-grandfather, the visionary Kgosi Khama III, Khama was a classic at heart. However, Khama remained grounded, contrasting his grandfather's aspirational ambitions. He was entirely focused on business when it came to getting things done.

Indeed, there were many political and economic turns for Botswana over the twentieth century, making it seem like a roller coaster ride. A constant, though, was the game-changing discovery of diamonds in the 1960s. Suddenly, Botswana found itself sitting on a mountain of riches, and with a little bit of luck and a whole lot of hard work, the country was poised for greatness. Since then, Botswana's leaders have been playing the long game, prioritizing growth, stability, and humility above all else. And what a return! Botswana was one of the leading African economies in 2021, with a GDP per capita of more than $18,113.

How did they do it?

Well, they put their diamonds to good use, investing in things like healthcare, education, and infrastructure.

But before then, the story of Botswana's economic history is characterized by shift and flow as reported by the World Bank. Remember that the year of independence, 1966, was marked by a consistent 6.344 percent economic growth, which was encouraging for a young nation. However, Botswana's ascent was truly remarkable in the early 1970s, when growth reached an incredible 26.362 percent by 1972. This surge pushed the country into the international spotlight.

The economic tide, however, started to turn. Growth rates began to level out in 1973 and progressively declined to 8.446 percent by 1975. A time of economic volatility, with occasional peaks and valleys, began in the years that followed. Significantly, in 1988, growth reached its highest point since 1972, reaching 19.45 percent; this demonstrates Botswana's ability to weather economic storms on a worldwide scale. But 2009 was the worst year for the economy ever, as it struggled with a slump that brought growth to a terrifying -7.652 percent, the lowest level ever recorded. Despite this setback, Botswana resumed its road to recovery and continued to make strides towards positive growth in the years that followed. On the verge of 2020, predictions indicate that it will recover from the depths of the recession that began in 2009. As a nation, Botswana has shown remarkable resilience throughout its economic path.

The year is 2023, and the diamond industry is now struggling. In the same year that Bloomberg reported on some lab-grown diamonds in the US, technology swiftly pounced on the business. Because of this, the value of rough diamonds went into freefall. We are putting aside the obvious reality that the pandemic has reduced demand for diamonds globally.

Regardless of these difficulties, the results will have far-reaching effects on the sector and beyond. As diamond prices continue to fall, traditional diamond manufacturers are seeing a decline in both revenue and profitability. And what exactly does this mean for Botswana? The simple reality is that if this trend continues, economic suffering will be worsened in places dependent on diamonds because of the widespread loss of jobs. Furthermore, development programs in diamond-rich regions, such as healthcare, education, and infrastructure, will be weakened by the economic slump because they were financed by diamond earnings. As a result, the diamond industry's problems have far-reaching economic consequences that affect adjacent sectors including jewellery production, retail, and tourism.

However, from the beginning, it has always been clear that Botswana has always been keeping their eyes on the prize, one of the wisest things Botswana did was to keep their debt levels low. Over time, Botswana managed to keep its national debt at bay, a feat that carries significant implications. Firstly, escalating debt tends to draw the government deeper into economic affairs, potentially limiting private sector innovation and growth. Secondly, higher debt levels often translate to increased tax burdens on citizens in the future, affecting their disposable income and overall standard of living. Additionally, having a clear plan for debt repayment is crucial for financial stability and long-term prosperity. Botswana's ability to avoid excessive debt accumulation has spared it from potentially dire consequences, showcasing its foresight and prudent financial management.

One of Botswana's secret weapons?

The Pula fund. Named after the Setswana word for "rain" – a symbol of blessings and good fortune – this rainy-day fund is where Botswana stashes its diamond riches. But it's more than just a piggy bank; it's a strategic tool, guiding the country towards economic security and prosperity.

The inflation rate history of Botswana is indicative of its flexible and resilient economy. The discovery of diamonds in the late 1960s stimulated economic growth and relatively constant inflation into the 1970s and early 1980s, following independence in 1966. But because of shifts in the diamond market, regional droughts, and worldwide economic swings, inflation rates spiked in the '80s and '90s. Inflation reached double digits around the time of the global financial crisis in 2008, a result of factors such as increasing food and energy prices around the world in the early 2000s. Inflation rates in Botswana reduced and remained within the 3-6% target range by the mid-2010s, thanks to the country's Central Bank's strong monetary policies aimed at stabilizing the economy.

Fresh economic difficulties emerged in 2020 due to the COVID-19 pandemic. Inflation was kept in check at first by reduced demand and cheaper energy, but it started to rise again in 2021 and 2022 when economies around the world started to recover, supply chains were shaken up, and commodity prices started to rise. As a result of both domestic and international factors influencing pricing in 2023, inflation remained a major worry. But Botswana's government and central bank have kept a sharp eye on inflation and have taken steps to stabilize the economy.

Botswana has shown economic maturity and strategic insight by taking proactive budgetary measures and diversifying its economy, which have been essential in managing inflationary pressures. This synopsis depicts Botswana's economic development through time, highlighting the country's resolve to maintain stability and progress in the face of changing circumstances.

And over the years Botswana's financial acumen hasn't gone unnoticed. Moody's, the big shots in the credit rating game, applauded Botswana, with an A3 from A2 credit rating and a stable outlook in 2021. Botswana is indeed showing the world that everything is achievable with planning and sheer willpower while facing obstacles like fiscal buffers and reliance on the mining sector.

But that's not all.

In the late 90s and early 2000s, Botswana had to face a harsh truth: it was the only African country fighting the overwhelming battle against the HIV/AIDS epidemic with the highest numbers and infact the highest in the world. Like an enduring shadow, this disease lowered the nation's hopes for progress and prosperity. Every part of society felt the effects of the far-reaching consequences. The demographic dilemma of a young, promising population threatened by a fatal virus was at the core of this catastrophe. Botswana had the difficult challenge of protecting its people's health and vitality while it faced the greatest HIV/AIDS prevalence on the continent. Surely this was a supreme anomaly! The effect was far-reaching. First, the country's hopes for development were put on hold by a rapidly spreading epidemic, which threatened to upset the delicate balance of population dynamics. The second impact of the epidemic was the generation of children who were left without parents and a clear path forward, all because of the virus.

And yet, through the shadows, light shone. The government of Botswana mobilized its citizens, gathered resources, and reached out to the international community to combat the disease. As time went on, combined efforts paid off, and the wave of infection waned, giving way to a rising wave of consciousness and strength. Botswana continued its road of resiliency and rebirth as word got out and shame started to fade. The country's ability to respond collectively to the epidemic demonstrates its dedication to protecting the health and welfare of its citizens. Botswana overcame challenges head-on, its resilience shining through as the country continued to make strides toward a better and healthier future.

Botswana's leadership, including figures like Seretse Khama, Ketumile Quett Joni Masire, Festus Gontebanye Mogae, Ian Khama and Mokgweetsi Masisi all played a pivotal role in steering the nation towards economic growth. The visionary approach of leaders like Khama and Ketumile Masire paved the way for Botswana's success, but they also recognized the importance of looking beyond diamonds and diversifying the economy to ensure a sustainable future. The economic success of Botswana is a tribute to the nation's many visionary leaders, who have all left their stamp on the country's history. Khama and Ketumile Masire are just two of the many remarkable leaders whose savvy leadership has been essential in guiding Botswana to economic success. Surely, the nation owes them a debt of gratitude for that.

These leaders bravely advocated for economic diversification after seeing the dangers of being overly dependent on diamond revenue. To ensure a sustainable future, they realized they needed to broaden their focus beyond diamonds and find other ways to advance. The leaders of Botswana had a vision, and with it, the country set out on a path of economic change, diversifying its revenue streams and preparing for long-term growth. Their vision and preparation have made Botswana an example of prudent leadership and economic stewardship for the region, and other countries want to follow suit. Beyond their official tenures, these leaders have left behind legacies of development and wealth that impact Botswana's path to a better future.

Did you know that Botswana has diversified its economy into sectors such as tourism, agriculture, and services, contributing to sustained economic growth and development?

Chapter Sixteen

The Botswana Stars-Athletes, Sports & Games

During my youthful days in Botswana, we would spend hours immersed in the joy of playing Morabaraba and diketo. These games held a special power to bring people together, creating a sense of unity and camaraderie. Morabaraba, with its African twist on the game of chess, offered a unique strategic challenge. We would carefully maneuver our game pieces on a distinct board, each move holding great significance, much like crafting a well-thought-out plot in a captivating story. On one hand, diketo was a game that demanded both skill and balance. Kneeling down, we would attempt to flip stones into various patterns, almost like a form of rock juggling. It was a delightful challenge that allowed us to showcase our abilities and enjoy ourselves in the process.

Morabaraba and diketo had a remarkable way of bringing families and friends closer together. They became vehicles for bonding and creating lasting memories. I can still recall those days when we would play these games endlessly, so engrossed in the competition that we would sometimes forget to eat. They were an integral part of our lives, connecting us to our heritage and fostering a sense of community.

In Botswana, various sports like table tennis, basketball, cricket, volleyball, netball, tennis, boxing, and more have gained popularity. However, it is soccer that truly captures the hearts of the nation. With each kick of the ball, a profound sense of unity and national pride reverberates across the land, connecting neighborhoods through a shared passion for the sport. The Zebras, Botswana's national football team, have become beloved figures, winning the hearts of the entire nation with their inspiring performances on the field. They embody the dreams and aspirations of every young football player in the country.

While the Zebras have enjoyed success in regional competitions, they have faced challenges when competing on the global stage. Yet, their unwavering determination and commitment never fail to ignite a deep sense of patriotism, fueling the nation's love for football.

Beyond the football field, Botswana has nurtured a remarkable lineage of exceptional athletes who have left an indelible mark in the annals of sports history. Take, for instance, Nijel Amos, who clinched a well-deserved silver medal at the 2012 Olympics, and Amantle Montsho, who ascended to the pinnacle of world champion status in 2011. Their awe-inspiring achievements continue to serve as a beacon of inspiration for aspiring athletes in Botswana, proving that dreams can indeed materialize through perseverance and steadfast resolve.

Another renowned figure is Isaac Makwala, whose name resonates with excellence and resilience. His momentous bronze medal win at the 2017 World Championships showcased the indomitable spirit that permeates Botswana's sports culture. Makwala's exceptional feats have earned him global acclaim, firmly establishing him as a genuine icon in the world of sports.

Botswana's athletes continually serve as a source of inspiration, uplifting their nation with their unwavering resilience, courage, and passion. They embody the rich sporting legacy of Botswana, carrying the hopes and dreams of an entire nation as they strive for success on the global stage. Their remarkable achievements ignite a collective sense of pride and togetherness that resonates deeply within every Batswana.

Letsile Tebogo has carved an extraordinary path in athletics, leaving an indelible mark on the sport and solidifying his place among the greats. With each gold medal he claims and every record he surpasses, Letsile becomes a beacon of inspiration for the aspiring athletes of the next generation, encouraging them to embrace their own potential and pursue their dreams with unwavering determination. He has achieved remarkable success, both on the local stage of dusty competitions and the grand international arenas.

Tebogo has displayed his lightning speed and unfaltering will on a worldwide scale, from becoming Botswana's Olympic representative in 2020 to setting World U20 records at the esteemed World Athletics U20 Championships. He solidified his role as a leader in Botswana's athletic environment with his 2022 African Championships silver medal and historic 2023 World Athletics Championships silver medal. Continuing his reign as one of Botswana's most illustrious sprinters, Tebogo won gold in the 100 and 200 meters at the 2024 African Championships. Letsile Tebogo is an example to young athletes in Botswana and abroad due to his extraordinary talent and relentless pursuit of achievement. He captivated audiences around the world.

Did you know that Kabelo Kgosiemang is a high jumper who has represented Botswana at multiple Olympic Games and World Championships? He holds the national record in the high jump.

Chapter Seventeen

Nurturing Ideas, Igniting Change- Innovation

The power of dreaming big lies in its ability to bring people together and enable us to shape the kind of community we've always longed for. I witnessed this transformative force during Botswana's pursuit of a more diverse economy. The strategic decision to shift focus from a heavy reliance on mineral resources, such as diamonds, to nurturing knowledge and innovation proved to be a brilliant move. Diamonds have played a significant role in Botswana's economy for a considerable time, and they continue to hold importance. However, by daring to dream big and embracing a knowledge-based economy, Botswana is opening doors to new opportunities and forging a future that aligns with its aspirations.

On a scorching July afternoon in 2014, as the sun beat down relentlessly in Gaborone, Botswana, my friend and I found ourselves driving through the city. The suffocating heat seemed to coax everyone indoors, seeking solace in the cool confines of their homes. However, our curiosity was piqued when we spotted a massive construction project taking shape in the vicinity of the Airport area.

The Botswana Innovation Hub was taking shape right before our eyes. This hub would serve as a haven for brilliant minds and imaginative ideas, a place where innovation could flourish. It was a thrilling realization that Botswana was on the cusp of a new chapter, poised for tremendous growth and boundless creativity.

When we reflect on Botswana's journey, it becomes evident that the nation has always been driven to shape a brighter future. It was their visionary thinking that led to the formulation of the Botswana Excellence strategy, a brilliant plan aimed at reshaping and expanding the economy, birthing the Botswana Innovation Hub.

In 2017, the Botswana Innovation Hub (BIH) officially opened its doors at the Science and Technology Park, embarking on a remarkable mission to establish it as it's first. This expansive park, spanning approximately 57 hectares, has attracted innovation-focused companies that have secured land to establish their presence. One of the primary objectives of the BIH is to contribute to Botswana's vision of achieving a knowledge-based status by 2036.

To fulfill this vision, the government took charge and commissioned a modern and well-equipped structure for the Botswana Innovation Hub, ensuring that it provides state-of-the-art facilities. This central meeting place has proven to be a valuable asset for the government, businesses, and universities alike. It serves as a dynamic hub where new enterprises can thrive, offering a conducive environment for research and development activities. The BIH goes beyond providing just physical space; it also offers essential tools, guidance, and financial support, empowering local innovators to transform their concepts into successful and sustainable ventures.

In 2020, it underwent a transition and emerged as the Botswana Digital Innovation Hub, playing a crucial role in digitizing the public sector. This well-orchestrated strategy has positioned Botswana as a hub of innovation, sparking excitement and opening a world of opportunities for the future. The Botswana Excellence strategy has the power to turn ideas into soaring realities, much like the origin story of a superhero.

As of 2023, Botswana has achieved a remarkable feat by securing the third position as the most innovative country in sub-Saharan Africa, according to the Global Innovation Index. This accomplishment is truly noteworthy and speaks volumes about the government's unwavering support. In fact, Botswana has gained recognition, ranking 27th among 33 economies in the middle-income bracket in terms of innovation. In a nutshell, Botswana has played a bigger role in creating a climate that nurtures innovation. Through strategic capacity development endeavors, Botswana has successfully cultivated a pool of skilled and experienced innovators who are driving technical progress and research forward.

The generous financing environment in Botswana has played a significant role in fueling innovation, too. It has provided crucial funding for research and development activities as well as the establishment of new ventures. This support has not only nurtured innovation and entrepreneurship within the country but has also attracted foreign partners and investors, further strengthening Botswana's innovation ecosystem. The country's devotion to innovation, despite its low ranking in the Global Innovation Index, demonstrates their unwavering commitment to research and development, technical advancement, and leadership. Botswana continues to shine as an innovation hub in Africa and beyond, thanks primarily to the government's unwavering backing. The favorable climate that promotes capacity development and provides financial help has created a fertile ground for innovation to flourish.

Private enterprises in Botswana have forged valuable partnerships with the government and the Innovation Hub, creating a mutually beneficial collaboration. Companies like the Letshego Group of Companies and Botswana Insurance Holdings Limited have played a pivotal role in encouraging young individuals to explore entrepreneurship opportunities by providing funding. Their efforts have opened doors for aspiring entrepreneurs, empowering them to take risks and pursue their innovative ideas. As someone who shares a deep passion for innovation, I have had the privilege of immersing myself in the vibrant ecosystem of competitions and hackathons at the Botswana Digital and Innovation Hub. It has been an exhilarating journey, filled with both triumphs and setbacks in which I won some competitions and failed others.

Botswana has embraced the power of technology as a spark for socio-economic progress. Initiatives like the National Innovation Competitions have sparked a wave of motivation among individuals to leverage technology and develop solutions that address community challenges. This concerted effort from the government has not only encouraged innovation but has also created a platform for individuals to make a meaningful impact in their communities.

Moreover, the government's commitment to digitalization and electronic governance has revolutionized public services, enhancing their efficiency and accessibility. Thanks to these advancements, registering a Botswana company has become a seamless process that can be done from anywhere in the world. The Companies and Intellectual Property Authority's digitization efforts have eliminated geographical barriers, making it easier for entrepreneurs to establish businesses in Botswana.

It's truly inspiring to witness the impact of mentorship and financial support provided by these institutions on the young generation.

Many talented individuals who have received such assistance have not only competed on international stages but have also achieved remarkable success, earning notable awards and recognition.

However, if we were to look at the situation from a different perspective, it would be disheartening to realize that these numbers of successful individuals are not increasing as rapidly as we might hope.

While the government of Botswana has made commendable efforts to foster innovation, it acknowledges that the country's advancement output falls below the average. However, this recognition has not deterred the government from actively seeking suggestions to enhance and broaden its innovation ecosystem. Understanding the importance of addressing this challenge, Botswana remains open to ideas that can drive improvement.

While Botswana acknowledges the need for additional funding for research and development, its progress in innovation is undoubtedly heading in a promising direction. The country is unwavering in its commitment to creating an environment that nurtures creativity, fosters collaboration, and positions Botswana as a leading center for innovation in Africa. Considering this trajectory, it becomes feasible and highly beneficial to establish more partnerships and implement additional projects. By forging strategic collaborations with both domestic and international entities, Botswana can leverage diverse expertise, resources, and perspectives to further fuel its innovation ecosystem.

Expanding partnerships and undertaking more projects will not only bring in additional funding but also facilitate knowledge exchange, promote technological advancements, and create fertile ground for innovative ideas to flourish. It is through these collective efforts that Botswana can continue to strengthen its position as an innovation powerhouse in Africa and achieve even greater heights of success.

Did you know that Botswana has been at the forefront of innovation in mobile technology, particularly in the area of mobile banking? The country's pioneering mobile banking service, known as "Orange Money" and "MyZaka," has transformed the way people access financial services, especially in rural areas where traditional banking infrastructure is limited.

Chapter Eighteen

Building Prosperity- The Institutions

As a country that has experienced exponential economic growth in the past, Botswana is a fascinating example of resilience, insight, and strategic genius. My interest in Botswana's growth has been piqued by learning about its humble beginnings, where struggle resonates against a backdrop of unlimited opportunity. Through its many twists and turns, this story brings readers to a world where the resilience of the nation is showcased in all its glory.

The leaders of Botswana showed remarkable bravery by refusing to be complacent in the face of such great challenges. Instead, they embraced diversification, propelling the nation towards a hopeful and opportunity-filled future. Even still, doubts are lingering in the halls of power, putting a damper on the successes. On the road to success, you have no idea what twists and turns you'll encounter or what results you'll get. Regardless, Botswana keeps its resolve strong, looking far into the future even in the face of adversity.

Did you know that Botswana offers a wide range of investment opportunities in industries including healthcare, education, mining, tourism, manufacturing, and much more?

It's fascinating to note that Botswana currently offers a wide range of investment prospects across various industries. Sectors such as healthcare, education, mining, and tourism are experiencing rapid growth and are ripe for fresh ideas and innovative approaches. Government actions and incentives are vital to establish a favorable climate for businesses. Botswana is well aware of this, which is why the country is making strides to attract and retain international investment. Botswana Investment and Trade Centre and SPEDU (Special Economic Zone Authority) are the conduits via which this is accomplished. SPEDU is a regional diversification program that is laser-focused on a small town that was formerly a prosperous mining town.

The country's attempts to streamline regulations and cut down on bureaucratic red tape demonstrate its dedication to making commercial operations easier. To streamline processes and reduce needless bureaucracy, Botswana is actively developing programs. The goal of the government's actions is to entice investors, especially in the banking and business services industries. These programs aim to lower the barriers to entry for new businesses so that they can boost the economy.

Looking ahead, Botswana is eager to embrace the future and welcomes investors who are interested in learning about and contributing to its diverse and expanding economy. As Botswana keeps trying to diversify its economy, the idea of New Economic Geography—as put forth by Paul Krugman—has taken root there. Because of its revolutionary potential to alter the country's economic scene, this proposal has sparked widespread enthusiasm. Companies in Botswana are excited to investigate this idea further in the hopes of finding growth potential.

When dealing with long-term objectives, it is even more important to establish and commemorate intermediate targets. One notable event that exemplifies this is the 2024 SPEDU Selibe Phikwe Citrus Project Harvest. Not only has this project created job and financial opportunities, but it has also opened the door for Botswana to start exporting citrus fruits to Europe.

At the core of SPEDU's approach is the skillful art of economic diversification, which involves creating a wide range of opportunities that extend far beyond the ordinary. They aim to revitalize the region by attracting investors and catalyzing economic growth. In essence, SPEDU acts as a conductor, orchestrating a vibrant trading and investing concert. But SPEDU's role goes beyond merely attracting investors. It can be likened to a regional playhouse, setting the stage for a revolutionary story. By strategically focusing on infrastructure development, SPEDU ensures that the necessary foundations are in place to support the region's economic transformation. SPEDU invites business enthusiasts to join them on this transformative journey, offering a platform where innovative ideas and strategic investments can flourish.

What's truly remarkable about SPEDU is that its mission extends far beyond physical infrastructure. It's all about nurturing the potential of individuals and ensuring that the local community isn't just passive observers but active participants in the economic transformation. Skill development lies at the heart of their efforts, empowering individuals and providing them with equal opportunities right from the start. SPEDU is like a financial genie, summoning funds from various sources to propel the region's growth. They're orchestrating a symphony of financial resources, not just attracting capital but ensuring that money flows in from all directions. It almost feels like they've mastered the art of financial wizardry. What sets SPEDU apart is not just their actions, but the way they carry them out, adhering to governance principles with flair. They resemble guardians of a corporate ballet, where every step is deliberate, every decision carefully timed, and the entire performance choreographed to the rhythm of responsible and appropriate leadership.

In essence, SPEDU goes beyond being a mere organization. It weaves a captivating narrative of the region's economic development, showcasing a harmonious transformation characterized by diversification, investment, skill development, equal opportunity, funding, and governance. It's a story that paints a vivid picture of success and growth.

Despite having abundant natural resources, such as 3,200 hours of sunshine per year, Botswana has been relatively slow in transitioning to renewable energy. However, there is now a significant acceleration in progress, particularly in the SPEDU region. In a remarkable stride towards sustainable growth aligned with its Vision 2036 objectives, Botswana implemented renewable energy solutions in mid-2022. A major milestone was achieved through a groundbreaking 25-year Power Purchasing Agreement between Botswana and Scatec, a renowned Norwegian energy provider. This agreement signifies a pivotal moment in the journey. It demonstrates the country's commitment to embracing clean energy and aligning with global sustainability goals. These remarkable efforts are perfectly in tune with the objectives, which sets the ambitious target of sourcing 50% of the nation's energy from renewable sources by 2036.

Teaming up with Scatec represents a significant leap for Botswana, as it embarks on its inaugural sustainable energy project. This strategic partnership signifies a pivotal moment in the country's journey to lower its carbon footprint and harness its abundant energy resources. The benefits that Botswana stands to reap from this endeavor are immense, ranging from enhanced technological capabilities to the creation of new job opportunities and overall economic growth.

This achievement truly showcases Botswana's determination to embrace renewable energy and actively participate in global initiatives aimed at combating climate change. Their eagerness to collaborate with organizations like Scatec and international partners demonstrates their proactive approach to finding innovative solutions to lessen the country's environmental footprint. Despite being endowed with a significant portion 66% of Africa's coal resources, Botswana's decision to undertake this sustainable energy project stands out as a remarkable testament to its commitment to global sustainability.

In a significant finding regarding the economics of trade openness, researchers have revealed that it can potentially lead to increased funding, optimal resource utilization, and the spread of new ideas and technologies. However, the impact of openness on economic growth is not as straightforward as initially believed. While it does play a role, it is not the sole determinant of growth disparities across nations. Other factors such as market dynamics and policies also significantly influence growth outcomes. Furthermore, there is an ongoing debate regarding the effects of trade openness on income inequality. Some argue that increased openness can exacerbate income disparities within developing countries. This complex interplay between the advantages and disadvantages of trade openness forms the core of discussions and negotiations between different perspectives, where rational analysis clashes with emotional sentiments.

Did you know that the Botswana Investment and Trade Centre (BITC) plays a key role in promoting Botswana as an attractive investment destination globally?

Chapter Nineteen

Shadows Of Progress- The Struggles

A major issue that keeps cropping up in Botswana is urban bias. It follows the country like a shadow, particularly when it comes to ensuring equality. It appears like there are a lot of opportunities and a lot of activity in the cities. But as you leave the city limits, a whole new world opens. Living in a rural region isn't always easy. Maybe you have a hard time obtaining work, and the nearest or best schools and hospitals are far away or just not available in these areas. Even so, it is intriguing to note that other nations, such as those in the West, have discovered methods to guarantee equal opportunity for all. This urban-rural gap remains a significant concern in Botswana. Things might improve if the country paid greater attention to the voices of rural residents. To ensure that no one falls behind, the nation can advance together if everyone has a say.

When tackling Botswana's infrastructure issues, it is essential to keep the political dimension in mind. Because decision-makers are more easily influenced by the views and demands of the urban majority, the voices of rural inhabitants are frequently ignored and overwhelmed during crucial decision-making processes. But if we want

Botswana to be a country where everyone can prosper, we must change our strategy. Stop making decisions in a vacuum and start treating people fairly; the moment has come. To achieve this goal, it is necessary to invest heavily in rural areas so that all people have a fair chance to prosper and to prioritize expanding access to healthcare and education for rural populations.

Income inequality is another major problem that Botswana must deal with. We are essentially borrowing from the future due to income inequality, which is a major concern. Our children, grandkids, and subsequent generations will have to pay the price for our inability to live up to our productive potential and for the unfair distribution of wealth. Inequality like this has the potential to cause future social unrest and diminished opportunity. Ensuring a better future for everyone is more important than simply being fair. Over time, the disparity between the rich and the poor has grown substantially, trapping the poor in a never-ending cycle of poverty while the privileged continue to accumulate wealth. According to specialists in the sector, this widening gap is worrisome and will have serious consequences for people who are already struggling to meet their most fundamental needs.

The plight of individuals who are unable to access necessities is truly distressing. It is during these moments that the importance of a strong social security net becomes evident. It seems like a lot of Botswana's problems stem from the country's income disparity. My observations and interactions with people in the country lead me to believe that this inequality has the potential to spark anger and resentment. One interesting thing to observe is that seeing other people living lavishly while others are struggling to achieve their basic requirements can make people feel angry. Anger and disillusionment can spread through a community when people's living conditions are so drastically different. Unfortunately, these kinds of situations can amplify existing societal problems, such as the proliferation of prostitution and an uptick in crime rates. Which have now become a reality in Botswana.

This situation reminds me of a controversy involving a law company. Massive documents leaked from a Panamanian law company, known as the Panama Papers. It showed how influential and rich people concealed their money in offshore accounts and avoided paying taxes. And the disgruntled anonymous whistle-blower stated that it is all because of income inequality. The rich kept getting rich while the poor kept getting poor. Like how Botswana's extreme wealth gap causes discontent and social problems, the Panama Papers revealed how the wealthy will stop at nothing to protect their fortunes, even if it means sacrificing public welfare. As with other forms of social unrest, the Panama Papers had their origins in injustice and inequality. These two instances highlight how critical it is to close the wealth gap through increased openness and equality.

It should come as no surprise that income inequality has far-reaching consequences beyond being solely a social issue—it has significant implications for the economy as well. When wealth becomes concentrated in the hands of a few individuals, a substantial portion of the population is left with limited purchasing power. This, in turn, has detrimental effects on businesses, leading to job losses and a negative impact on the overall economy.

A large disparity in income can also reduce the likelihood of long-term economic expansion. When opportunities and resources are limited to a small percentage of the population, a lot of unrealized potential goes unused. Everyone from individuals impacted to companies and the country at large is losing out in this circumstance.

So, what are the possible solutions?

Well, when it comes to addressing income inequality, the question of potential solutions carries considerable financial implications. We need to improve productivity, and this is the path to sustained prosperity. And how do we do that? One proposed approach is to prioritize increased investment in education and healthcare, recognizing the significance of providing equal opportunities for individuals to succeed. Botswana's educational system must improve in areas like vocational training and helping young people identify and develop their unique strengths. Our nation has a huge unrealized potential when it comes to vocational training, which might produce a new generation of hardworking, competent people. The education in this field is unfortunately not up to par, thus many people go into vocational schools more as a pastime than as a means to an end (real employment or making good use of their abilities).

To that end, many people have difficulty putting their education and skills to good use after finishing their studies. The continual requirement to import workers from Zimbabwe is making this situation even worse. If Botswana's vocational education system is to provide its youth with a real chance at a prosperous future, these shortcomings must be eliminated. The value and importance of vocational education should be acknowledged.

Providing people with opportunities to explore and participate in real-world professional experiences and mentorship is crucial when they are thinking about their future careers. By giving people these chances, we can help them find their passions and develop their skills through real-world experience in a variety of industries. By taking this route, people are better equipped to learn about themselves and choose careers that play to their talents and ambitions. In the end, encouraging realistic job assessments helps people make educated decisions about their future careers. This way, we are not left in a frightening predicament of having leadership and skills deficits because of today's work practices. There is a lot that Botswana can take away from the educational systems of countries like Japan, South Korea, and Canada, which are renowned for their high-quality education systems, rigorous curricula, and stellar performance on international assessments. Botswana can get valuable insights from these nations regarding how to enhance its educational system and improve academic performance. Some people think that wealth distribution should be more equitable, and they advocate for policies like higher taxes on the wealthy and social welfare programs to help the poor. In my opinion, raising taxes on the wealthy could discourage investment and entrepreneurship, two factors crucial to economic growth, if left unchecked. Some individuals might want to put their money into investments abroad, for example.

While it's true that social welfare programs benefit those who truly need them, many worry that recipients may become dependent on the system and less likely to put effort into improving themselves or finding gainful employment. They think it's important to help people in need while also promoting individual initiative and responsibility. The long-term viability of social welfare systems is another issue, especially in middle-income nations like Botswana which have limited resources. Supporters may stress the need for policies that encourage economic independence and self-sufficiency, while still offering specialized aid to those groups most in need.

The government of Botswana deserves praise for its programs that promote equitable economic development. Some worry, meanwhile, that these programs aren't helping small businesses and the lower class as much as they could. There is a gap between the intended beneficiaries and the method of delivery based on my experience and conversations with folks trying to use these resources.

This is very worrisome because low-income communities and small businesses have distinct issues that need individualized solutions. They might not have the same perspective on opportunities or knowledge of how to deal with bureaucracies as other parts of society, such as graduates. So, if you don't tailor your approach to their thinking and situation, just giving them tools or help might not cut it.

Policies that provide these groups with real and lasting influence should take precedence over taxation and social assistance programs as the only means of redistribution. Mentorship, training, and individualized support networks are all part of this, in addition to financial aid. And it should be done right. More just and prosperous outcomes can be achieved for everyone if we listen to the voices of the marginalized and craft programs to help small businesses and the poor.

Regardless of the specific solution, one thing is clear: income inequality is a pressing issue that Botswana cannot afford to overlook. To build a stronger and more prosperous nation that benefits all its citizens, it is crucial to confront these disparities head-on and ensure equal opportunities for everyone to succeed.

Over the years there has been a lot of debate among scholars about Botswana's welfare regime, with different perspectives shaping the narrative. Some people see it as a minimalist welfare state, with a narrow focus on targeted interventions. On the other hand, some critics have called it conservative, pointing out perceived weaknesses in addressing wider social needs. The heart of this discussion revolves around the way welfare is provided in Botswana. The focus has mainly been on helping the poor, especially those who are most vulnerable, like orphaned children. This focused approach demonstrates a purposeful decision to tackle pressing socio-economic issues among the population. By giving priority to supporting the most vulnerable, policymakers aim to address immediate hardships and promote social cohesion. Despite these commendable efforts, there are still lingering questions about the adequacy and inclusivity of Botswana's welfare regime. Although social assistance programs have undoubtedly helped many people in need, there is still a portion of the population who are stuck in extreme poverty and are not able to access these benefits. This difference brings up some important questions about how well the current welfare systems work and if they help everyone who needs it. In addition, the limited reach of Botswana's welfare system highlights the larger structural inequalities and systemic barriers that impede access to social support. Various challenges, like being far away from resources, dealing with red tape, and facing societal biases, can make it difficult for marginalized people to get the help they need. This can keep them trapped in poverty and isolation.

Given these challenges, it's clear that Botswana's welfare regime needs some serious reform to make things fairer and more inclusive. This involves not just increasing the reach of social assistance programs, but also tackling the root socio-economic inequalities and giving marginalized communities the power to fully engage in the development process. In the end, the discussion about Botswana's welfare regime highlights the intricate relationship between policy decisions, socio-economic conditions, and the pursuit of social fairness. While experts analyze and discuss its effectiveness, it is crucial to create a welfare system that ensures nobody is left behind and respects the dignity and well-being of all citizens.

The traditional circle that opens comparison in welfare regimes, is Botswana and Mauritius. Why would I want to compare Botswana with Mauritius? It is because these two countries seem like two peas in a pod, but when it comes to welfare policies, they take different routes. Mauritius has a wide range of social assistance programs that demonstrate a dedication to providing support for everyone and fostering social unity. On the other hand, Botswana's welfare initiatives have a more specific focus, aiming to support vulnerable populations such as orphaned children. The variations in these aspects underscore the intricate relationship between political, economic, and social influences that shape welfare policies in different countries. Still, we must not forget the difficulties we encounter, especially concerning cost. Some academics are worried that Botswana won't be able to afford to continue and even increase its welfare programs. To build a better, more equitable future for all Batswana, we must address these concerns and come up with creative solutions.

Moreover, Botswana must continue to engage in thoughtful policies that bring the benefits of free trade in the Southern African Development Community (SADC) region and internationally. As a member of SADC, which is headquartered in Gaborone, Botswana's capital, and the African Continental Free Trade Area (AFCFTA), two trade agreements that aim to promote economic growth and regional integration. Botswana is targeting investment, increased competitiveness, and commercial opportunity via tariff reduction, customs procedure streamlining, and support for export-oriented companies. Thoughtful government regulations that encourage entrepreneurship, and the growth of SMMEs are important because they create much-needed competition in our economy. Competition drives efficiency, innovation, and economic growth in the economy.

Now, the question arises: Is Botswana genuinely committed to advancing its economic status and improving social welfare?

Without a doubt, by looking at the past, we can gain insights into what we can expect in the future. When we review the developments and strategies being implemented in the next ten years, we can anticipate nothing short of astonishing progress.

Achieving these goals necessitates substantial investment, unwavering dedication, and consistent prioritization from top-level leadership. Like any endeavor, those who put in the effort can expect the rewards to be within reach. It's a matter of recognizing that the path to success requires commitment and perseverance. By staying committed and making the necessary investments, Botswana can unlock the potential for a prosperous future that benefits all its citizens. The efforts made today will lay the foundation for the rewards that lie just around the corner.

To achieve our objective, it is crucial to enhance access to high-quality education and career training, particularly for our younger generation. Our primary goal should be to improve our strategy by incorporating active labor market policies, inspired by the successful practices of countries like Norway. By doing so, we can provide vital support to unemployed youth.

This comprehensive approach goes beyond simply helping young individuals secure jobs. It also involves offering free essential services such as career counseling and interview preparations. It's important to recognize that expecting job seekers to pay for these services with limited financial resources is not practical. Instead, we should consider implementing these services nationwide, ensuring that all young people have equal access to the support they need to succeed in the job market.

I envision the implementation of a groundbreaking Youth Guarantee program and employer subsidies as significant steps forward. However, the top priority should be the nationwide provision of these essential services. By prioritizing this approach, we can establish the foundation for a resilient, equitable, and prosperous society.

The plan is simple yet powerful: ensuring that every young person within our borders has access to opportunities for employment, education, or training. This comprehensive approach will leave no one behind, offering a pathway for all young individuals to thrive and contribute to our nation's development.

In this journey of progress, it is crucial to remain dedicated to learning from the experiences of world-class welfare providers. By studying their mistakes and successes, we can continuously refine our own strategies and policies. Botswana has the potential to become even better, building upon the lessons learned from those who have excelled in providing comprehensive welfare support.

Chapter Twenty

The Beginning To An End

Indeed, an African success story, having stepped into the middle-income bracket in 1986, Botswana rose to the upper-middle-income bracket in 2005. Botswana also gained recognition for its political stability and economic growth over the years. Democracy and fiscal responsibility in government have brought the nation praise from around the world. Everyone seems to agree that democracy is based on a few fundamental principles, even though their exact definitions may differ. Among these, we find safeguards for minority rights, free and fair elections, human rights, majority rule, and consent of the governed. With these cornerstones in place, Botswana is a model of democratic values.

Important characteristics of Botswana include a long history of peaceful elections, a fair judicial system, and the rule of law. Because of these traits, the country is known as an example of African democracy. A dedication to democratic principles is demonstrated by Botswana in its upholding stability and fairness for all inhabitants. Being acknowledged as a democratic leader not only elevates Botswana's status but also forces the nation to uphold and advance democratic principles. Botswana's commitment to democratic rule is a statement about the importance of diversity, equality, and human rights.

Beyond its political stability, Botswana achieved remarkable success by implementing a game-changing factor. But what was the game changer?

It became evident that being democratic and having well-designed institutions alone would not suffice to effectively manage resources and achieve significant accomplishments. Economists widely acknowledge that policies play a crucial role in fostering growth and progress. These policies encourage stability, creativity, investment, and efficiency, which are vital for long-term development. The effectiveness of these institutions is closely intertwined with the broader social and political landscape in Botswana. The country enjoys a vibrant community, characterized by active public discussions and energetic grassroots movements, such as the Kgotla meetings. Additionally, there is a diverse range of accessible media platforms that contribute to an open and informed society.

An example of Botswana's collaborative approach and strong partnerships is the 10-year diamond sales deal signed in 2023 between the Botswana Government and De Beers for Debswana's raw diamond output. This agreement also extended the mining licenses for an additional 25 years. This significant step forward signifies the close collaboration between Botswana and De Beers, with both parties working together to finalize agreements that will enhance Botswana's diamond industry. The agreement covers various aspects, including financial arrangements, the establishment of the Diamonds for Development Fund, supply allocation, talent development, and growth of the value chain. This partnership between a government and a multinational company is a first of its kind, highlighting the mutual benefits for both Botswana and De Beers.

Such collaborations demonstrate the commitment to leveraging Botswana's diamond resources for the benefit of its people. The agreement reflects the government's dedication to fostering economic growth and development through strategic partnerships and effective resource management. Despite its small population, Botswana boasts a diverse political landscape, with four distinct political parties represented in the current national parliament. This multiparty system ensures a variety of perspectives and voices are heard in the country's political decision-making processes. The media landscape in Botswana is equally vibrant, with approximately ten newspapers providing a platform for a wide range of viewpoints to be expressed and disseminated. This diversity of media outlets ensures that citizens have access to different sources of information and can engage in informed discussions about various issues.

In addition, Botswana's governance structure reflects a decentralized approach. The presence of over sixteen district councils highlights the country's commitment to devolving power and decision-making authority to local levels. The dynamic and diverse society in the country plays a crucial role in shaping the ever-changing landscape. It is within this intricate web of various groups and individuals that an important task emerges – the close scrutiny of institutions, their decision-making processes, and resource management. Civil society, comprising a multitude of voices and perspectives, actively engages in the evaluation of these institutions. They provide valuable feedback, ensuring fairness and balance in the functioning of Botswana's governance.

This collective effort helps to maintain accountability and continuously improve ideas and practices over time.

The result is a strong and adaptable system where excellent ideas and practices are more likely to be adopted and sustained, while problematic approaches are thoroughly scrutinized and exposed. This democratic system not only fosters accountability but also empowers the people to question and demand transparency. Therefore, the success of Botswana's resource management cannot be attributed solely to its institutions; it is equally influenced by the active participation of its diverse civil society and the presence of platforms for public discussions.

Botswana has gained a well-deserved reputation for its unwavering dedication to integrity and its tranquil and secure atmosphere. The country is widely recognized for its exemplary ethical governance, characterized by a strong stance against corruption, a robust legal system, and an unwavering commitment to upholding the rule of law. One notable evidence of Botswana's promise to creating a trustworthy and business-friendly environment is its consistent ranking as the second least corrupt country in Africa, as indicated by the Transparency International Corruption Perception Index. This ranking reflects the country's persistent efforts to combat corruption and maintain high ethical standards. Furthermore, Botswana's economy has been acknowledged for its commendable level of economic freedom. In 2023, the country was ranked 52nd in terms of it by the Heritage Foundation, with a score of 64.9.

Botswana's economic growth and progress have been significantly influenced by its commitment to maintaining an open economy. The country has actively engaged in foreign markets, emphasizing trade and investment as key drivers of development. Leveraging its abundant natural resources, particularly minerals, Botswana has utilized these assets to fuel economic expansion.

Through trade partnerships with countries worldwide, Botswana has expanded its market reach, enabled the export of its goods while gaining access to a diverse range of products and services from other nations. This exchange has facilitated economic growth and fostered mutually beneficial relationships. Foreign direct investment (FDI) has played a pivotal role in Botswana's growth trajectory. These investments have contributed to the establishment of new facilities, the creation of employment opportunities, and the transfer of valuable technology. By attracting FDI, the country has not only boosted its economy but also enhanced its capacity for innovation and development.

While Botswana's open economy has propelled its progress, it has also exposed the country to various risks and threats from the global arena. This highlights the importance of implementing smart policies and diversification plans to ensure a strong and stable economy in today's unpredictable world. By mitigating vulnerabilities and embracing strategic measures, the country can safeguard its economic well-being and navigate potential challenges.

In summary, Botswana's dedication to an open economy has been a fundamental driver of its growth and development. By actively participating in foreign markets, emphasizing trade, and attracting foreign direct investment, the country has positioned itself as an active player in the global market. The story of Botswana embodies resilience, visionary leadership, and a steadfast dedication to unity and progress. Starting from its humble beginnings as a land rich in diverse indigenous cultures, grappling with poverty, to its transformation into a shining example of hope and advancement in Africa, Botswana's history exemplifies the remarkable potential of human determination and collaboration.

Throughout its journey, Botswana has encountered challenges and obstacles, but it has consistently demonstrated resilience in overcoming them. Guided by visionary leaders, the country has embraced a long-term perspective, implementing strategies that have fostered sustainable development and improved the lives of its people.

As I reflect on my journey, I find many parallels between Botswana's story and my quest for knowledge and understanding. Like the nation, I have faced challenges and endured moments of doubt and hesitation that nearly derailed my progress. I have shown up exhausted and messy yet determined. I showed up before I was ready, openly sharing my struggles and fears. I have shown up imperfect and scared. The key is that, just like Botswana, I have shown up consistently and authentically. My journey isn't about achieving perfection; it's about embracing reality.

Did you know that Botswana is one of the few countries in the world where the majority of its land is dedicated to national parks, reserves, and wildlife management areas?

Chapter Twenty-One

Author's Note

Growing up in my homeland, I was immersed in a culture of resilience, community, and progress despite the many challenges we faced. Yet the outside world seemed to know little about our true story and the ambitions we hold. As an African who has witnessed immense transformations across the continent, I felt compelled to share our inspiring journey - how we have overcome immense hardships through unity and visionary leadership.

In writing this book, I have aimed to paint a vivid yet balanced portrait of Africa - one that celebrates our diversity while also acknowledging the problems that still linger from colonialism, corruption, and other traumas inflicted upon us. I have drawn from my own experiences visiting different nations, as well as interviews with leaders, businesspeople, artists, and everyday citizens. I hope that by giving a human face and voice to Africans, readers will develop a deeper empathy for our shared struggles and a greater appreciation of the untapped potential across the land that I am proud to call home.

Above all, I wish to tell the story of my homeland - the "Secret Jewel" that has managed to stay stubbornly under the radar despite its invaluable lessons of strength, progress and what a community can achieve when it remains unified in the face of adversity. It is a story I dedicate to my son Emil, for whom I hope this labor of love will help ensure that Africa's future generations feel proud of who they are and are empowered to build an even brighter future.

Printed by Amazon Italia Logistica S.r.l.
Torrazza Piemonte (TO), Italy

60470914R00077

THE SECRET

In her insightful debut book, **Peggy Morris** takes rea Africa to uncover the remarkable story of her homelar **"The Secret Jewel."** Through vivid prose, Morris paints a portrait of a nation that has weathered immense challenges throughout its history yet remained resilient through visionary leadership and a commitment to unity.

Morris explores the cultural and economic diversity across Africa, highlighting the distinct traits of various nations while emphasizing the common threads that unite the continent. She discusses the long-lasting impacts of colonialism and the lingering problems of corruption. She also profiles success stories, such as Rwanda's economic rise and feminist leadership. For Morris, she believes Africa's future remains bright if the potential of its diverse talents and untapped resources can be fully realized.

Woven throughout are the author's own experiences that have shaped her perspective. You will be guided on a journey of discovery about the true character of Africa, and a treasure hunt to find a particular nation that has stayed stubbornly in the shadow. For anyone seeking to understand Africa beyond preconceived notions, this book shines much-needed light on the little-known **"Secret Jewel"**, and its indomitable spirit

ISBN 9788269374810

90000

9 788269 374810